The Thought of Contemporary Spanish Essayists

Edited and Translated by
Donald W. Bleznick
University of Cincinnati

UNIVERSITY
PRESS OF
AMERICA

Lanham • New York • London

Copyright © 1993 by
University Press of America®, Inc.
4720 Boston Way
Lanham, Maryland 20706

3 Henrietta Street
London WC2E 8LU England

All rights reserved
Printed in the United States of America
British Cataloging in Publication Information Available

Library of Congress Cataloging-in-Publication Data

The Thought of contemporary Spanish essayists / edited and translated
by Donald W. Bleznick.
p.   cm.
1. Spanish essays—20th century—Translations into English.
I. Bleznick, Donald William, 1924–   .
PQ6267.E8T56   1992   864'.608—dc20   92-24203 CIP

ISBN 0–8191–8860–3 (cloth : alk. paper)
ISBN 0–8191–8861–1 (pbk. : alk. paper)

  The paper used in this publication meets the minimum requirements of American National Standard for Information Sciences—Permanence of Paper for Printed Library Materials, ANSI Z39.48–1984.

Published with the help of
The Charles Phelps Taft Memorial Fund,
University of Cincinnati

CONTENTS

PREFACE

PEDRO LAIN ENTRALGO Today and Tomorrow	1
JOSE LUIS ABELLAN Spanish Exile in Contemporary History	17
FRANCISCO AYALA	29
The Rise and Fall of Modernity	30
To Enlighten Public Opinion	33
Language, Literature and Politics	37
ELIAS DIAZ The New Social Pact: Political Institutions and Social Movements	41
JOSE JIMENEZ LOZANO The Danger of Reminiscing and the Ensuing Tales	53
JOSE CARLOS MAINER Literature in the New Democratic Society	69
XAVIER RUBERT DE VENTOS	79
From Nationalism to Nuclearism	80
Imbroglio and Development	85
Encounters in the Labyrinth	90
FERNANDO SAVATER The Future of Ethics	95
EDUARDO SUBIRATS Screened Existence	109
EUGENIO TRIAS The Beautiful and the Sinister	119
BIOGRAPHICAL SKETCH OF EDITOR	133

PREFACE

For about five hundred years Spanish cultural life has suffered from a negative public opinion that has thrived in Europe and other Western countries. The terrible events of the national Spanish Inquisition that began in the late fifteenth century were instrumental in causing the rise of the "black legend" which has survived to this century. Over the centuries Westerners had come to criticize Spain for its religious intolerance and the harsh methods it used to eradicate heresies, for the morally offensive conquest and colonization of its territories in the New World, and for its cultural and artistic deficiencies. Until quite recently, Spain was considered to be an isolated appendage of the European continent.

We may consider late 1975 as a significant watershed since at that time Francisco Franco died and his 39-year-old dictatorship ended. Not long after constitutional monarchy was formed and Spain has also become a full-fledged member of the European community. Although Spanish culture and Spanish writers and artists become better known abroad earlier in this century, the last 15 years have seen a greater awareness of Spaniards' contributions to European letters and culture.

As a Hispanist who has devoted more than 40 years in academe to teaching and writing books and articles and presenting papers on Spanish literature, I have publicized in the United States and abroad the treasures of Spanish literature and the stimulating ideas generated by Spanish minds. It is through this volume that I wish to demonstrate to an English-speaking audience insufficiently conversant with Spanish culture, history, literature, philosophy, art and aesthetics, that today's Spanish writers are indeed on the cutting edge of contemporary Western thought and that their uniquely original and exciting insights into their own and universal history of ideas and cultural accomplishments demand that what they have written be more widely known.

This book had its genesis about two years ago. After much correspondence with potential authors and colleagues who know the authors included in this collection, essays written by ten of the most distinguished living Spanish writers were selected. These authors range in age from the mid-forties to the mid-eighties and although they are from different generations their essays share the commonality of being up to date and fresh. Four essayists wrote pieces expressly for this collection and the other six are represented by writings that have been published within the last few years. Information on the essays in this volume is provided below and bio-bibliographical data on their authors will be found at the end of the book.

I decided to put Pedro Laín Entralgo's essay first since it is broader in scope that the others and serves as a fitting introduction to the entire collection of essays found in this book. The other essayists are presented in alphabetical order.

Pedro Laín Entralgo, former president of the Spanish Royal Academy of Language, anthropologist and emeritus professor of the history of medicine at the University of Madrid, is one of Spain's most eminent Spanish intellectuals of this century. His fascinating essay deals with man's present-day life and the problems man will face in the next century. In his "Spanish Appendix" he sounds a rallying call to Spaniards to fulfill themselves in the future through self-analysis and self-reform.

José Luis Abellán, who has written extensively on Spanish history of ideas, philosophy and sociology, writes in his previously unpublished essay about the uniqueness of Spanish exile and the toll that it exacted on Spanish writers during and after the Spanish Civil War (1936-39), and especially the effect it had on Juan Ramón Jiménez who received the Nobel Prize for Literature in 1956.

Francisco Ayala, member of the Spanish Royal Academy of Language and one of the outstanding Spanish novelists of this century, muses about where postmodernity may lead us, the effect that television has on the masses of people and the attitudes that government and individuals have taken with regard to the minor languages (notably Catalan and Galician) versus the dominant Castilian language in Spain. He shows how language can unify and separate the people of a country.

Elías Díaz, who holds the chair of the Philosophy of Law at the University of Madrid and has written numerous books and articles in his fields of interest, proposes a new social pact based on democratic legitimacy and justice, a system of government that must allow criticism and self-criticism in order to be viable.

José Jiménez Lozano has published several books of essays on Spanish literature and art as well as seven book-length narratives. The unpublished piece submitted for inclusion in this volume is a brilliant study on recapturing the past through narratives and art. He utilizes many sources from European literature and history as well as his profound knowledge of art to comment on the "authentic" lot of common people in different ages since biblical times.

José Carlos Mainer, a prolific historian and literary critic, writes about culture and literature in democratic Spain. He finds that despite the accessibility of reading material, the educational system has not sufficiently prepared students to read and, consequently, young people are more attracted to visual images and loud music. This is obviously a universal complaint.

Xavier Rubert de Ventós, professor of aesthetics at the University of Barcelona, former member of the Spanish Parliament, elected member of the European Parliament, and author of 15 books in Castilian and Catalan, is represented by three essays: on nationalism and nuclearism, and two pieces on the nature of the Spanish colonization of the New World and what the United States can learn from the Hispanic experience.

Fernando Savater, professor of philosophy at the Universidad del País Vasco and one of the most brilliant and prolific of the young Spanish philosophers, who has written more than 40 books and is well known throughout the Hispanic World, has contributed an unpublished essay on the future of ethics. Following a stimulating discussion of what ethics means, Savater turns to Jose Ortega y Gasset's belief in order to "increase the ethical ideal" we must be "constantly prepared to make "reforms and corrections." He concludes by citing Ortega's statement taken from his *Meditations on the Quijote:* "Every system of ethics which orders the perpetual imprisonment of our free will within a closed system of evaluation is ipso facto perverse."

Eduardo Subirats, another of Spain's leading philosophers, is very much interested in aesthetics. He has been a visiting professor at Princeton University (1990 and 1991) and in several Latin American countries. He has written several books on philosophy and a prize-winning study on postmodernism. His study on "screened existence," a thought-provoking essay on the role of spectacle in modern society, was originally written for this volume.

The final essay, was written by Eugenio Trías, a professor of aesthetics and composition at the School of Architecture in Barcelona. He has written a dozen books on a diversity of themes and is considered to possess one of the best minds among the young Spanish philosophers. Trías is represented by most of the first part of the second edition of his best-known book *The Beautiful and the Sinister* (1988), which won the prestigious National Essay Prize. One of the intriguing conclusions of this dazzling essay, which is buttressed by graphic examples taken from life and literature, is that "the beautiful, without mentonymical reference to the sinister, lacks the force and vitality to be able to be beautiful."

I have learned how arduous and demanding the art of translation is when one is concerned about belying the old Italian dictum that "translators are traitors." It has been my abiding aim to be as creative as possible in stretching my mind during the task of translating into English the original thoughts and ideas of ten of the most outstanding Spanish intellectuals who are still writing. These writers and American colleagues familiar with their writings have encouraged me to pursue this endeavor and to them I am most grateful. Furthermore, I wish to thank all the writers in this collection for graciously granting me permission to use their material as well as the following people for their generous help in assembling the contents, in helping with the translations and in processing the manuscript.

I am greatly indebted to Professor Thomas Mermall of Brooklyn College, an outstanding scholar who made invaluable suggestions regarding authors who might be included in this book and helped and encouraged me throughout the whole process. Professor Nelson Orringer of the University of Connecticut, an exceptionally knowledgeable and meticulous scholar in the 20th-century Spanish essay, generously provided useful suggestions and was instrumental in enabling me to find a suitable essay by Pedro Laín Entralgo. Roger Llopis Fuentes, a talented Cuban writer and translator, spent a good deal of his time checking my translations and generally aided me in the editing of the manuscript. I wish to express my special gratitude to Phyllis Oberacker, whose computer skills and patience were essential in preparing the manuscript for the camera-ready stage.

Cincinnati, Ohio   December 24, 1991

PEDRO LAIN ENTRALGO

Pedro Laín Entralgo was born in Teruel in 1908. He studied chemistry and medicine in several Spanish universities and later in Vienna where he did postdoctoral studies in psychiatry. During the years 1951-56 he was Rector of the University of Madrid. He was the first person to occupy the chair of the History of Medicine at the University of Madrid a post he relinquished when he was around eighty. Until recently he was the president of the Royal Spanish Academy of Language and also a member of the Royal Academy of Medicine. He has published a vast number of books and essays on such topics as the history of medicine, philosophical and medical anthropology, Spanish history and culture, and Spanish literature and literary figures. Some of his important non-medical books are: *España como problema (Spain as a Problem)* [1948], a long study which discusses Spain's inability to become a modern state while attempting to remain true to its Catholic roots; *La espera y la esperanza (Expectation and Hope)* [1957], a theory of hope based on the premise that hope must exist in order that mankind may accomplish things, and *Descargo de conciencia (1930-1960) (Unburdening My Conscience)* [1976], Laín's personal history of the events that took place principally during the Franco era. Laín has received France's prestigious Montaigne Prize and several honorary degrees from the University of Toulouse, the National University of Santiago in Chile and the University of San Marcos in Lima. He also has membership in many European and American societies and academies.

TODAY AND TOMORROW

Today

Man lives essentially and inexorably within a world, even when he wants to become an ascetic dwelling in a wasteland or when he is namelessly forced to live in an urban ant-hill. In this world he may or may not see his own residence, "his house." When will his world be his house? Undoubtedly, when he sees as "his own" the totality of all kinds of social habits--mental, technical, political, aesthetic, including those related to his self-esteem--that are part and parcel of his life. If I am transplanted to Tibet, my world will be Tibet, but not my house, although Tibet is where I eat, sleep and think. If I imagine as an historian the life of a Greek *polis* while I am submerged in the task of reconstructing it and understanding it, I am making the Greek *polis* my world. But no matter how great my love for ancient Greece is, only when I return to the things, the people and the habits of my daily existence--my city, my acquaintances and friends, the events that the daily newspaper publishes or advertises--do I go from being the most devoted lover of Greece to one of its most unhappy abhorrers. Only then can I say that I am in my historical abode, and consequently in my present-day temporality. This temporality is the totality of social habits of every kind, by virtue of which I historically exist in my world as in my own abode. The question now is to know when Western man began the life that he considers to be current, that is, his historical present-day temporality, and to know what are the fundamental characteristics of this temporality.

I. A great mental effort is not necessary to take stock of the relativity and conventionality of the concept of "the historical present." The ambience of this concept varies, indeed, with the age of those who express an opinion on this subject--a youngster, an adult and an aging individual are of a different mind as to that which is of current actuality--and with the culture to which they belong. What is current to a farmer can be out-dated in the eyes of the inhabitant of the large city. This also holds true for that which refers to the substance of an opinion. Although a technical gadget and a philosophical system (or, perhaps a novel) simultaneously come into being, they do not remain on the same footing; the gadget can become obsolete while the philosophical system may remain current. But it is also certain that with the many reservations one might conjure up, the average man of a country, or a whole cultural ambience, knows what things are about when he speaks of "my time," and when one speaks to him of the "present-day" or of "present life." With this in mind, we ask when the present day began for a man of the 80's.

In order not to get lost in vague remarks, let us look for the response by examining some of the fields in which man's historical life comes into realization and is expressed. Present-day architecture--that of New York's Park Avenue, that of Brasilia--began with the Bauhaus of Weimar and Dessau, and afterward came the concordant creative work of Gropius, Le Corbusier, Mies Vander Rohe and Frank Lloyd Wright. Painting became formally present-day with the full maturity of Picasso and with the actuality and universality of Kandinsky and Mondrian. Modern philosophy began with phenomenology and its ontological consequences (Husserl, Heidegger, Sartre), neopositivism (Carnap, Schlick, Wittgenstein), the global zenith of Marxism, which followed the October Revolution and World War II, and metaphysical speculation in the aftermath of this multifarious and complex experience of the human mind. The physics of today began with the universal diffusion of quantum and relativity theories, and with the later creations regarding the applicability of Rutherford's atomic model (Bohr, Heisenberg, Schrödinger, Broglie, Fermi, Dirac). Modern psychology stems from the decline of Wundt's work, and the worldwide recognition of Freud. Current literature springs from the explosion of literary "isms" and their later consequences. The great upheaval in technology arises from the utilization of atomic energy, coming after those huge discoveries in physics, with the scientific planning of space flights--Hans Tirring and others initiated it more than 50 years ago--, and with the invention of the computer (during the decade of the 30's). The general style of life, when social rigidity and artificiality of the *belle époque* were substituted in the entire West by sports and the juvenilization of living. "Comradeship. Down with conventions!" the German youth shouted around 1920. There is one conclusion to be arrived at from this kaleidoscopic examination: culture began to be "current" for us in the period after World War I, that is, in the decade spanning the 20's.

Yes, from that time on, historical life for Western or Westernized man took on a present-day configuration. Let us try to discern with certain precision the fundamental traits of that life.

II. Many will judge such an undertaking to be non-viable. They will say, for example: "Between an orthodox Marxist of Moscow and a Christian capitalist of Boston, between a Sicilian farmer and an Osaka industrial worker, is there perhaps a similarity other than that of being men, traveling in automobiles or on planes and wearing garments that are analogous to a certain extent?" But I dare to think that if all those men are moderately educated, something similar must be in their heads and in their hearts beneath the clothing they have in common. From being a theological postulate (St. Augustine, St. Bonaventure, Boussuet) or a philosophical concept (Hegel, Comte, Marx), the "universal history of humanity" has come to be a real fact for three reasons: 1) because the technology of communications today allows the news about some event to touch within a few hours the hearts of all, or of almost all the inhabitants of the world; 2) because the technique of aggression makes possible the destruction of the most far-off city in a short span of time; and 3) because--and this is the decisive thing for us--the awareness of our being involved in the plot of a common historical destiny has penetrated more and more deeply the existence of men at this juncture of the 20th century, whatever the nationality and the religious and political creeds may happen to be among men. Here are some of the fundamental traits of this awareness and this common destiny.

1. *The transition from the personal experience of the crisis as a novelty to the experience of the crisis as a habit.* Except for some highly perceptive minds, like those of Nietzsche, Dilthey and Unamuno, men before World War I firmly believed that humanity, supported by the capacity of its reason to govern its own reality and that of the world, advanced and was going to continue advancing along the broad road of progress. For them, the wars and revolutions would be nothing else than brief painful episodes in the course of that ascending march, occasional disorders of a promising constant and indefinite growth. It was then that thrived, to use a topical expression, the *belle époque.* As it came to pass, despite the optimism of the Europe and America of the "happy twenties," the terrible experience of the two world wars were to reveal, as a bitter and alarming novelty, that an epoch of universal history, the modern world, had entered a crisis, and that the armed conflict of 1914 had only been a bloody expression of that enormous critical event. José Ortega y Gasset was to write that a crisis exists when man lacks historical beliefs upon which his existence is based, and from that perspective several famous essays were written about the situation in which Western man found himself: Spengler's *The Decadence of the West* (1918), Berdiaeff's *A New Middle Age* (1924), Jasper's *The Spiritual Situation of Our Time* (1931), Ortega's *Change and Crisis* (1933), Huizinga's *Among the Shadows of the Morning* (1935), etc. The intellectual, a supreme witness of the situation in which he exists, has become confused, disoriented and very unhappy as Zubiri observed in 1942. Confused, because the different sciences lack clearly defined characteristics and a hierarchial order; disoriented, because on a great number of occasions he does not know what to do with the truths he has discovered, or because he limits himself to use them without understanding them, discontent because the roots of his knowledge do not penetrate to his soul. Such come to be the respective consequences of the three main orientations of thought at the dividing point of the 19th and 20th centuries: positivism, pragmatism and historicism.

Up until this point, we have all the consequences that are inherent in life in a critical situation--alarm and disorientation, constant repudiation of the immediate past, a tendency to feign and indulge in self-deception, disjointed sentimental impulses, versatility, according to Ortega's description--, the discovery of the crisis as novelty and thereafter, in the wake of World War II and its immediate sequels, the personal experience of the crisis as an historic habit. For present-day man, whether or not he hopes that the 21st century may bring to the world a well-established "new order," whatever it may be, to live socially and historically is to live in crisis. This seems to be the root from which germinate the tensions of collective life, the general spiritual disposition of almost all human beings and the occasional events which, without becoming apocalyptic, have so repeatedly and deeply upset us. It is a generational conflict, a rebellion of young people, outbreaks of violence, disinterest in face of the immediate world, the rise in the use of drugs, anguish in face of the contamination of natural resources, disorder in the historical integration of the people of developing nations, oppression of the weak by the strong, etc. Hegel might have said that humanity has not gone beyond the stage of "unfortunate awareness" without failing to believe in progress and to work on its behalf. Many present-day men, less optimistic than Hegel, live with the thought, or act as though this were what they think, that the "unfortunate awareness" constitutes a spiritual habit of our existence in the world.

2. *The extreme secularization of historical existence and a new attitude toward man's possibilities vis-à-vis the world.* The secularization of historical existence, the resolute will to live based only on natural reason and only within sentient reality is certainly not a new matter. It began in the 18th century and continued to make great progress in the 19th. Around 1900, almost the whole proletariat and most intellectuals of the West tried to live their lives in a secular fashion. Hegel and Nietzche, each one in his own way, had proclaimed the death of God. What is pertinent to our time is not secularization, nor even its enormous ascendancy, but the enormous change in perspective that has been brought about regarding its anthropological and historical sense. Indeed, a goodly number of secularized people has begun to feel that the habitual secularization of life is compatible with a certain religiosity, and many believers have begun to think that secularized historical existence is not in itself a religiously "pathological" existence; in other words, the secularization of life must belong in some way to the normalcy of existence in society and in history. The Englishman's credo, wrote Alasdair McIntyre, a well-known sociologist in the field of religion, is that there is no God, but it appears sensible to pray to Him from time to time. Using the word "God" in its broadest sense could not but constitute a stroke of ingeniousness in the eyes of any one who did not wish to be misled from the path of a key understanding of the spirit of our time.

In nature, as learned medieval men put it in their translations from the Greeks, there are two categories of necessity: *absolute necessity*, in the presence of which man's technical resources are of no avail, and *conditional necessity* which belongs to the sphere of the human and thus is amenable to man's control. Already in the 14th century that doctrine began its theoretical decline with the development of voluntarism and nominalism. Condorcet, at the end of the 18th century, stated that "nature has not put limits on our hopes." To illustrate this conviction with an appealing example, he added: "It is undoubtedly true that man will not become immortal; but the distance between the moment in which he begins to live and the epoch in which naturally, without illness, he feels the difficulty of being, can he not ceaselessly continue to grow?" Only in our time, when scientists have begun to control the conversion of matter into energy, when organs are transplanted, when substances that do not exist in nature are artificially manufactured, when there is scientific control over heredity, when animal behavior is controlled from a distance and the artificial production of organic life does not seem so remote, has the awareness of that lack of limitation become solid and universal. "What is not possible today will be possible tomorrow" is the belief of everybody, which alludes to the almost infinite possibilities of man facing the cosmos rather than to the exercise of God's infinite power.

3. *The will of plenitude in scientific knowledge and the awareness of its penultimacy* or the barriers perpetually standing in the path of ultimate knowledge. That will of plenitude is seen in two ways: one that deals with the historical point of view, and the other that concerns the method applied to this point of view. The former consists of keeping in mind the whole past in the configuration of the current work. The immense historiographical work of the last two hundred years has allowed us to understand with previously unknown subtlety and depth all the human situations of the past; but this understanding, involving the intellectual probing of the *raison d'être* and the historical sense of any situation and any work, can be exercised with historicist intention or assumptive intention. In the first instance, the expert historian of the past exhausts himself contemplating its marvelous diversity, and as Dilthey did, typifying it according to a system of conceptions of the world; in the second instance, he tries to assume originally in his own work the many and partial reasons for the existence of that whole past. For example, present-day anthropological medicine tries to assume, on a higher intellectual and practical level than that of Hippocrates, Galen, Paracelsus, Mesmer, Claude Bernard, Virchow and Freud. But also, from the point of view of method, the will of plenitude is applied, from which there results the essentially multidisciplinary character of current scientific knowledge, the substitution of the isolated researcher by the team or, on the other hand, the universal validity which so many in our time have given to Bohr's famous principle of complementariness.

This will of plenitude has been reversed and is combined today with a general awareness of the penultimacy of scientific knowledge. Science for men of the preceding century, was a knowledge of salvation, and the quasi-priestly ethos of the learned men of that time made them see it this way, a fact which may be found in reading the obituary Virchow wrote in honor of his master Johannes Müller. For present-day men, on the other hand, science does not go beyond being a knowledge of the intellect, and of power; and consequently, unlike yesteryear's priestly learned men of science, those of the present time have taken on the guise of the sportsman, that is to say, of a person whose vocation is devoted to the accomplishment of penultimate goals with regard to what the sense of human existence ought to be in itself and in its pursuits. This ambiguity of method, simple agnosticism and the more or less firm belief in some of the various formulations of that sense--Christian, Marxist, etc.--are the most frequent expressions of that general awareness of the penultimacy of our knowledge.

4. *The universalization of the two great revolutionary ideals of the modern world.* Beneath the diverse doctrines by means of which the several revolutions of the modern world have been or may be interpreted, it is hardly necessary to point out that Marxism-Leninism is the most important

and widespread of all of them. These revolutions have had two basic ideals: civil freedom (the effective possibility of living one's life in the world according to each one's personal beliefs, whatever these may be) and social justice (the habitual fulfillment of natural rights to enjoy in sufficient measure all the good things that nature affords and man's creative activity can offer). One of the main characteristics of current historical life consists of the universality of both ideals. There are persons and human groups in which the ideal of liberty stands out, and there are others in which the ideal of justice predominates. There are, finally, countries and occasions in which the two ideals are sorely wounded, but the diverse de facto situations do not take away universality from their complementary validity. Whether he is white or black, religious or atheistic, an inhabitant of the northern or southern hemisphere, present-day man feels himself, and as such is defined, as aspiring through peace or war to achieve both social justice and civil liberty, all the while with the hope--more often than not, under the weight of a vivid awareness--that achievement of justice and liberty will soon become an historical reality.

5. *The aspiration of making the future predictable.* The need to count on an image of the future to make worthwhile the life of the present, essentially pertains to Man's existence. Under the form of a project, the future is essentially in the present just as individual existence is in that of collective existence, but never has there been so much intensity as today in the desire to foretell the future, and never has the aspiration been so energetic to arrive at its image in a methodical and scientific way. "What will tomorrow be like?" Victor Hugo would ask himself, and then with the resignation of a conquered titan, he would end up saying, "But you, man, will not wrest tomorrow from Eternity." Today's response is very different. In applying his secret eagerness to achieve technical omnipotence, present-day man, besides expressing himself imaginatively, under the form of science-fiction, that deep need of his spirit tries to calculate by extrapolation the immediate future (hundreds of sociologists, statisticians, economists, biologists, engineers and doctors of the entire world are working on the task of knowing through calculations what human life will be between the years 2000 and 2050) and conjecture what in the distant future, through the work of biological evolution, can be the reality of the human species (see, for example, the book *The Next Million Years* written by Charles Darwin, the great grandson of the author of *The Origin of the Species*.) The presumptuous technical word "futurology" has been invented to designate that tough scientific exploration of the world's near and distant future.

6. *The general organization of life according to the urban model.* During several centuries the human habitat has been divided into two contrasting modes, "the city" and "the country" with the consequent stereotyping of the individuals as "city" man and "rural" man, has been central to the sociological description of the lives of people. In the early years of this century, there were hardly any Western countries, including those which were "developed" as we are wont to say today, in which that division of human beings did not have a patent reality, although the term "citizen" was indiscriminately

applied to them all in the text of the laws or in the language of the politicians. In fairly recent years, two enormous historical events, the ceaseless growth of the large cities and the generally increased use of technical advances in everyday life--concomitantly, the ever growing utilization of public and private transportation, the electrification of the home even in the smallest towns and isolated farms, the general diffusion of movies, radio and television, etc.,--have been organizing collective existence according to a rational and uniform urban model. It is certain that the difference between the city and the country still continues, but each day it is becoming less, and not only regarding dress, locomotion and recreation.

    7. *The demographic explosion and the biological sufficiency of natural resources.* In the epoch of Tiberius, the population of the world did not go beyond 50 million inhabitants. If from that time on it would have increased only at the reduced rate of 0.5 per 100, in Napoleon's time the planet would have been inhabited by more than 400 billion inhabitants, that is, about 120 times more than the totality of people who are living today. Epidemics and diseases, as well as hunger and war, have prevented this from happening. Despite the mortalities that modern wars have produced, during a little more than a century the rate of growth of the population has been increasing and we have every reason to believe that the more than 4 billion inhabitants of our time will rise to 6 or 7 billion in the year 2000. Two questions arise nowadays in the minds of thousands of our fellow humans: will the resources provided by nature and technology be sufficient to feed and clothe that immense and growing multitude of human beings? And, will society's masses, so vigorously described by Ortega more than half a century ago, increase in the same proportion?

    III. The passage from the experience of crisis as a novelty to the experience of crisis as a habit, the extreme secularization of existence and a new attitude vis-à-vis man's possibilities in the world, the will to seek plenitude of scientific knowledge and the awareness of its penultimacy, the universalization of the two great revolutionary ideals of the modern world, the claim of making the future predictable, the general organization of life according to the urban model, the uneasiness in face of the consequence of the population explosion are some, if not all, of the fundamental characteristics of current life, under the diverse national and ideological attitudes which contend with one other or are integrated in that life. This is tantamount to affirming that such characteristics acquire concrete reality through vital attitudes that are very different and sometimes hostile one to the other. Such attitudes can be arrayed according to three main points of view: sociopolitical, intellectual and religious.

    1. *Sociopolitical diversity.* From a sociopolitical point of view, the two poles between which man in our time is situated are integral liberalism (of which the system of free enterprise is an economic result) and pure socialism (or the stratification of nationalized property and credit at the base of the economic system). These poles are not as far apart as it would seem, for there are multiple possibilities mediating between them; today, impinging along their lines, there are concrete forms of common political life. Will the

immediate future hold in store a cycle of intensified socialization in liberal countries, and will it broaden the channel of freedom in socialist countries? This is the most desirable and seems to be the most reasonable of the current sociopolitical possibilities of our world.

2. *Intellectual diversity.* Two other opposite poles may be discerned in the uneasy and varied intellectual life of our time: the negation or the indifference in face of all that is not a perceptible fact, a representative symbol of it or a rational combination of such symbols in the form of scientific law (a demythicized and unsystematic enduring symbol, as a pure and simple mentality, of the *esprit positif* of Auguste Comte), and the conviction that a transposed, metaphysical mental attitude is necessary to make an intellectual account of reality, whatever may be the concrete form of this attitude, the content of the assertions to which it leads, the degree of evidence with which these assertions are imposed and the depth of our acquiescence to them. Without touching upon whether the question of Marxist vision of the world is dialectical, purely scientific or contained in a metaphysical latency which advertises itself as materialistic, in keeping with the dualistic precedent set by the theoretical skein of most of the intellectual movements of our world, to wit, Marxism, neopositivism in its different forms, structuralism and the various metaphysical constructions now in vogue.

3. *Religious diversity.* The brief preceding note about the magnitude and sense of the current secularization of life is not by itself sufficient to understand, even in a schematic way, the religious situation of the world to which we owe our existence. It is, indeed, necessary to discern in it three attitudes vis-à-vis the ultimate sense and ulterior consistency of reality: theism, atheism and agnosticism. A spiritual theistic attitude is expressed by those who believe and think that cosmic reality and human existence possess a foundation which transcends them and causes them to exist. The atheistic condition is demonstrated by those who in one way or another think and believe, because without belief there is no true atheism. In this regard, Unamuno's sonnet "The Atheist's Prayer," deserves to be read, as well as Zubiri's essay "Concerning the Problem of God." And with greater or less proximity to the deism of the philosophers of the Enlightenment, or to Comte's faith in the Great Being, agnostics can be defined as those who, with intellectual frivolity in their conduct or with anguish in their private lives, never decide to run, according to the famous words of Plato, the "beautiful risk" of believing in the existence or non-existence of that last foundation of what is real. Let the sociologists of religion tell us how the totality of the men of our time are distributed along these three cardinal lines of religiosity. I see humanity's current life as being unitary and diversified.

Tomorrow

The passage from today to tomorrow is an adventure--*ad ventura* means "toward what will come"--both in essence and etymologically. No matter how scientifically rigorous futurologists may be, as Victor Hugo's foregoing turn of phrase reads, their prognostications do not any the less stand at variance with the imponderabilities of *ad ventura*. Man's adventure consists of projecting the future by recalling that part of the past which the execution of each projection seems to require. Tell me what you are looking for and I will tell you what you remember; tell me what you remember and I will tell you what you are looking for. It is true that men look for more than what they project; it is likewise true that our memory contains much more than what we need to remember. To exist in time is to plot real paths and possible paths within the infinite scope which, taken together, provide or impose hope and nostalgia, repentance and fear. But only in becoming an adventure, a risky and inciting project, does human hope take tangible form.

The preceding section of this essay states how I see our historical situation, our today. If what one expects or fears as far as tomorrow is concerned contains what is seen and what is remembered in the present as its main focal point--according to Ortega, memory is the ladder that man uses to climb to the future--the key of all that I am going to say now is found in what I have said until now. What man thinks and knows about himself, about his present reality, is only a reflexive preparation--or a hectic preparation if you will--of what he is prepared to do. Pre-paration and also pre-occupation. To be preoccupied is to be occupied with what tomorrow will be. As Zubiri said, one prepares to be when one asks oneself at the same time what will happen to one. Let us see, in a very synoptic way, the structure and the contents of present-day man's preoccupation with his future.

I. Our most immediate preoccupation regarding tomorrow seems to be composed of six main themes: food, education, work, leisure, knowledge and power. In the year 2000 when six billion people will be living on the face of the earth, how will that swarm of people be able to feed itself? How will education be and what will each one of that mass of humanity be on top of what their life will demand of them? What will their work be? How will they fill their leisure time which their technological inventions are already beginning to make available? What will humanity know about the themes that already disturb us now? What will man be able to do regarding his own reality and world reality? Our hope for the future in the making tells us man in the year 2000 will have enough to eat, he will see his social differences diminish, he will work more rationally and productively than today, he will use his leisure time appropriately, he will know things we scarcely suspect today, and he will be capable of doing marvelous things for himself and the world. But at the very core of our hopes for future times, the subtle stimulus of fear makes us think of the following matter: since man is capable of madness, who can rule out the possibility of a thermonuclear catastrophe? And since he is capable of stupidity, who will be able to prevent him from running the risk of becoming an ant?

Let each man's thoughts be what they may. As far as I am concerned, hope prevails in my soul. I am far from accepting doctor Pangloss' rosy optimism. Unfortunately rose is not the only color of life. Egoism, sorrow, stupidity and injustice will always exist in life. That is true, but not to the extent that these attributes dominate those elements in life that are not injustice, sorrow, egoism and stupidity. Earth will not be a paradise in the year 2000 but neither will it be a wasteland in which the terrified few men who have survived a war of self-destruction of the human species wander senselessly about. No, I cannot believe that the three most central conquests of the twentieth century can constitute an event which is both fleeting and inane. I refer to the creative character of technology, the imperative of achieving a harmonious relationship between freedom and justice, and the awareness of man's unlimited power vis-à-vis nature.

II. I must return to a brief development of the ideas on modern technology which I outlined in the first part of this essay. *Recta ratio factibilium*, the "straightforward reason of doable things," is a renowned scholastic dictum that can be applied to art and technology. The ancient Greeks thought and believed that in nature there are "inescapable or fatalistic things," *anánkai*, which are absolutely beyond the power of man to transcend. Three of those inexorable natural inevitabilities are: human beings are mortal, stones fall, and the sun rises in the east and sets in the west. To try to fight against these uncontrollable phenomena would be plain stupidity or the flagrant sin of arrogance. In Christian terms, this conviction constitutes one of the strengths of the medieval definition of art.

But history did not end in the 13th century. By virtue of the turn of events regarding man, the Christian conception of man that began to take place toward the end of that century, Western thought would come to realize that for the human spirit there are no absolute needs in nature, at least that there are none in principle. Man's limitations in face of nature are de facto limitations and not made by law. What is not possible for man today will be possible for him tomorrow if he tenaciously applies his intelligence and effort. Under the form of a utopia this is the abiding sense, like the first babbling of what later would be called the "fortunate spirit" in Roger Bacon's *Republic of the Faithful*. Centuries later, when the modern world came into being, Descartes was to propose to man the splendid goals reserved for his earthly adventure: in knowing the force and actions of fire, water, air, the heavenly bodies and of all the other bodies which surround us ... we could become as owners and possessors of nature," he tells us in his *Discourse on Method*. The expeditious enjoyment of all the fruits of the earth, the conservation of health, the certainty of an old age free of infirmity and weakness, all this and much more will be attained if the *Discourse* is correctly used. Influenced by Descartes, Fontenelle was to write a little later that thanks to good method and awareness the ingenuity of men has already accomplished memorable deeds; and in what constitutes an openly prophetic turn of mind, he adds: "and it is evident that all that has no end." The idea of an indefinite progress in man's knowledge and power vis-à-vis nature has been firmly implanted in European minds.

Let us now leave the examination of what the idea of progress has been in the modern world, and let us ponder again the innocent faith of the enlightened people of the 18th century in the progressive moral political and artistic perfection of humanity. What can we, who lived in the time of concentration camps and gas chambers, think of that faith? Regarding knowledge of and control of nature, can we not view those men as the precursors or dreamers of the epoch which is now beginning?

Until our time, the limitless possibilities of technology in the best of cases did not go beyond the thought of a few doctrinaires. Today, when man has walked on the moon and science-fiction is simultaneously a pastime and a prophecy, things have begun to change in a spectacular way. Let us examine whether this is the attitude of our minds vis-à-vis the three inescapable natural phenomena mentioned previously.

The sun rises in the east and sets in the west. Does it not seem to be a notable foolishness or madness to think that this fact is not always an inexorable inevitability for man? It is true. In all probability, men, until the human species becomes extinct, will continue seeing the rising of the sun in the east and its setting in the west. But is this by chance an absolutely physical necessity? Can we not imagine a change in the dynamics of the solar system which will alter what has seemed eternally immutable until now? And does not man's technological intervention in the disintegration of matter, and as a possible consequence in the reality of the solar system, make conceivable the modification of such dynamics? It does not seem to be an absolute impossibility then that humankind, through its technology, can alter the place where the sun rises.

Stones fall: falling--to fill what is "below"--belongs to the nature of the stone according to the ancients. Is this so? At the present time man is already capable of carrying stones to a region of the cosmos in which they fly and do not fall. And, moreover, is it not conceivable to imagine a physical system in which gravity, considered universal until now, is an entirely different phenomenon from what it is on earth?

The mortality of living beings. This inevitability seems more urgent now. Condorcet's words--"there is not doubt that man will not become immortal"--must be repeated today. Men die and they will continue dying. But if man's science and technology are not capable of overcoming man's mortality, is it not certain that they have already begun to control the moment and the chance of death. Although they are still in their early stages, hibernation and organ transplants have become part of man's social myth. After so many centuries of intense practice in the art of killing, men have eagerly begun to practice the very new and captivating art of not dying.

III. From dominion over the cosmos, let us turn to man's own life. By means of the convulsions and anguish of our day, will men find themselves somewhat nearer the ideal of justice and liberty which the thinkers of the 18th and 19th centuries predicted? Perhaps. It is certain, in any event, that sorrow will continue to be mixed with happiness and pleasure in the existence of Adam's children. Let us remember once again Azorín's splendid paragraph on Garcilaso's "sad feelings": "Eternity, unfathomable eternity of sorrow. The human species will progress marvelously, it will accomplish profound transformations. Near a balcony, in a city, in a house, there will always be a man leaning his meditative and sad head on his hand. Nothing will wipe away his sad feelings." Yes, that is certain, because liberty is an essential part of the human condition, and because anxiety and waywardness inexorably belong to the exercise of liberty. Among many other things, to be a man is to be able to fail, to live straddling the promise of creation and the threat of ruin, to be at the same time--this is the most disquieting thing--*homo creans* and *homo labens* ("a creative man and a destructive man").

Azorín's aforementioned text can be presented in two different ways. It may be stated: "The human species will progress marvelously, the profound transformation will be accomplished, but man's sad feelings will not be wiped out." Nothing is less doubtful. On the other hand, it may be stated another way: "Man's sad feelings will not be wiped out, but the human species will be transformed in the profoundest way and will progress marvelously." The social perspective of hunger, war, disease, injustice and pollution vouches for the use of the first version; the confidence in the growing development of science and technology validates the second. It is perhaps not fair to divide humanity into two groups which correspond to those two ways of understanding the relationship between progress and sadness. I belong to the second group.

More than 100 years ago, the poet Baudelaire looked at the various windows of his being and confided in us the result of his experience: "I only see the infinite through all the windows." What was Baudelaire contemplating that made the word "infinite" the ultimate key of his version? The matter is clear to many: he was contemplating the modern world, and within it, its protagonist, modern man, a man who in his reality and his worldly life has undergone the experience of limitlessness and cannot renounce it.

There is nothing more revealing about this than the words of Heidegger, the greatest proponent of the finitude of existence, at the end of his book on Kant: "Does it make sense to conceive of man, on the basis of his most intimate finitude, as *creator* and therefore *infinite*? Is it right to hold this idea? Can the finitude of existence, even as a problem, be developed without a presupposed infinitude?" Like Baudelaire, although less intuitive and more cautious than he, Heidegger looked at the window of his reality, his "existence," and discovered the infinite in it.

Let us leave intact the serious metaphysical problem set out by Baudelaire's verse and Heidegger's questions. Let us concentrate only on what is historical life, an adventure toward the future, in human existence. For present-day man, what is the guiding force of that adventure? I remember a photograph of New York City's Empire State Building which had the following inscription on its foundation: "America, the country of limitless possibilities." That inscription applied to the whole world could be today the motto of humanity. "Earth, the planet of limitless possibilities." Would these expressions make sense if they did not incorporate the desire for and the awareness of infinitude?

Caution: I am not trying to affirm that man's power over nature lacks limits. How could that not be since man is a corporeal entity by his own nature and is therefore obliged to exist in space and time? The ancient Greeks had a reason to teach that nature imposes inexorable and inescapable limitations on mortals. But modern man has discovered that those inescapable limitations are fundamental in him and are not cast in empirical mould. Putting it another way, man's inventiveness will be reducing more and more, in an unlimited way, the scope of what seems to be an invincible must. Until yesterday, to see what there is on the other side of the moon seemed a completely physical impossibility, but today it is an accomplished fact. For surgeons of half a century ago, the transplanting of a human heart was only the dream of a visionary, but it has been done in recent times. In the exploration of the cosmos and in the management of human life, what will be the ultimate and definitive possibility? If not the infinite, we must bear in mind that what is unlimited is on the other side of our windows when we peer at the future through them.

I have just cited Baudelaire. Since the prophet is the one who prophesies, it may be opportune to end this essay on the possibilities of our tomorrow by giving universal scope to a stanza written by the Spanish poet Antonio Machado:

> What importance does a day have! Yesterday is open
> to tomorrow, tomorrow to the infinite.
> Men of the world, neither the past has died,
> nor is tomorrow--or yesterday--written.

Yesterday is not written because each era understands the common past in its own way. For us, Greece is at the same time the "Greece of us all," stretching back to Cicero to take in Burckhardt, and "our Greece," that peculiar Greece of present-day men. Tomorrow has not been written of because we and our children will be the ones to write about it day by day. Nevertheless, we do know something about that tomorrow. With its sorrows and its glories, its splendors and its blemishes. it will cover a limitless horizon, at least for men whose ambitions are not subject to the constraints that reaping the day's livelihood put on them.

Spanish Appendix

This is the way I see the current historical situation of humanity and the important traits of the near future. Within this future, and keeping in mind that each country participates in its own way in the common history of the human species, what form will Spanish life take, being as it is a Western country situated in the geographical crossroads of Europe, Africa and America? How will the Spaniards--to whom Antonio Machado's previously cited stanza was addressed--write their not as yet written tomorrow? I do not know. I only know that the answer will depend on our collective conduct vis-à-vis the three traits of our people I described above, traits which in Spanish society have only very partial reality.

1. The secularization of historical existence. Let us look at the composition of our society from this point of view. On one side are those who through sincere conviction or tactical decision--i.e. because they understand what exactly they must think as Spaniards--judge as formally anti-Christian the secularization of earthly life. On the other side are those who equate Christianity's attainment of secular fulfillment with an anticivil and ultramontane agenda, meaning by this the upholding of papal authority over national or diocesan authority through whatever means the church must use. It is certain that the number of those who find themselves between both extremes is becoming greater. I do not believe, nevertheless, that that number is sufficient for a satisfactory and efficient adaptation to the today and the tomorrow of the Western world.

2. The will of plenitude in scientific knowledge. In a country like Spain, which is so far from dedicating to science the intellectual esteem and economic attention which seems unavoidable in the West, can that trait of present-day historical existence be considered a social fact? Has science been for the average Spaniard--except for small worthy groups--what it should be in the second half of the 20th century? Consequently, should it not be admitted that in Spanish society there is a shortage of love for reason and rationality of which our governing minorities must take stock marshalling the willpowers to undertake vigorous reforms?

3. The social experience of the two great revolutionary ideals of the modern world, civil liberty and social justice. For reasons closely connected with the contents of the two preceding paragraphs, a good part of our society does not sufficiently value the good that civil liberty brings and not enough of our people intimately feel the imperative of social justice. There is a new need for self-analysis and self-reform.

The theological argument *potuit, decuit, ergo fecit* ("he was able, he made up his mind, therefore he did it") has been attributed to the philosopher Duns Scotus, apparently without any basis. Whether this attribution is legitimate or not, let us apply it, by secularizing and futurizing it for what is held in store for Spain, and for her ability to prove herself adequate to the rules laid down by Western countries that are in the vanguard because of the strides they have made in their quest to carry forward. Our motto should be "it can be, it must be and then it will be." If all Spaniards who aspire to utilize their ability to read and think make this their slogan it is certain that its prediction will become a reality. Let us attain our goal.

[Translation of essays taken from *Teatro del mundo* *(Theater of the World)* (Madrid: Espasa-Calpe, Colección Austral), 1986]

JOSE LUIS ABELLAN

José Luis Abellán was born in Madrid in 1933. He received his doctorate in philosophy from the University of Madrid in 1960, specializing in the history of ideas in Spain and Latin America. He currently holds the chair of the history of Spanish philosophy at the Universidad Complutense of Madrid where he also teaches the history of American ideas. Abellán has lectured at a number of institutions in Spain, Europe and America. Among his most important works are books on Unamuno, Spanish philosophy in America, the sociology of the generation of 1898, Spanish erasmism, and the monumental *Historia crítica del pensamiento español (Critical History of Spanish Thought)*, a five-volume work published between the years 1979 and 1988. The National Prize of Literature (1981) is one of several prizes he has won.

SPANISH EXILE IN CONTEMPORARY HISTORY

Exile is a socio-political phenomenon of the contemporary history of Europe, which includes an element of political will that does not exist in the phenomena of other periods whatever similarities may be present. Expulsion, exile, proscription or deportation cannot be compared with exile since the former are depotic acts on the part of one whose tenet of power lacks legitimacy and who in the exercise of such power undermines the self-will of the governed. One exception may be the case of emigration, but although self-will exists in this case, it is evident that it does not have a political character for it comes from other causes which may be mainly work-related or economic.

As far as Spain is concerned, it is known that exile constitutes one of the characteristics most repetitively found during the contemporary period, so much so that one could say that our history is, from its very beginnings, a history of exiles. It is necessary to look for its causes in the political conditions with which Spain initiated its modernity toward the end of the fifteenth century. This modernity resulted from the Spaniards' struggle during the Middle Ages against the Islamic invasion, which shaped a political structure--the first modern state it has been said--based on the religious unity of Catholicism, which in turn caused inevitable problems in terms of living together, for peoples who were not of one faith, which happened with Jews and Moslems.

Both these peoples were irrevocably expelled, the Jews in 1492 and the Moslems in 1609. This was the end result of the sweeping and unstoppable policies engineered by a Catholic State. This set into motion what present-day historiography has aptly termed "inquisitorial mentality," whose immediate manifestation as attested by the political conduct of the leaders, boiled down to a single criterion, namely that of persecuting, and exterminating the dissidents. These are the reasons which explain the difficulty of bringing forth a modern State based on a liberal creed, which quite naturally implies tolerance for dissenters, for opponents and even for adversaries.

It was inevitable then, these being the foundations, that the contemporary period would find difficulties, oftentimes insurmountable in its ability to conform to structures that have characterized European modernity. Therefore, the struggles between liberalism and absolutism repeatedly broke out during the ninteenth century in the armed confrontations known as the Carlist Wars. It is true that the Inquisition had disappeared definitively in 1835, but the "inquisitorial mentality" persisted in the minds of Spaniards, and those who lost the war knew that. They were condemned to become expatriates unless they were willing to risk their lives. This is the reason why the history of the past century was filled with exiles, Carlists or liberals, and the reason why these exiles were linked with the army, for in view of the non-existence of the Inquisition, the army came to embody the very attitudes which were characteristic of the "inquisitorial mentality." The lack of historical perspective of this development could very well be viewed as a monstruous abnormality, since national sovereignty was monopolized by the military if not subjugated by it.

This situation reached its apotheosis in the twentieth century during the bloodiest civil war that has ever taken place in our land: that of 1936-39, which determined the division of Spain into two irreconcilable factions. Because that civil war meant a total territorial schism in the country, wherein there were no geographic spaces or zones which remained marginal to the conflict, we can understand precisely why the term "the geographics" was applied to those who were on the side of one or the other faction and were so aligned on account of the mere fact of living in a given physical locale at the outbreak of the civil war and not on account of their sentiments or their ideology. The Spanish Civil War implied a total commitment and the impossibility of remaining out of the conflict affected even those who consciously fled it, who departed from the country without taking sides. The dialectic established by the war prevented these Spaniards from accomplishing their desire and they were automatically classified as a "Third Spain." Moreover, there was another decisive factor in the spread of the conflict, which was its growing internationalization and the resulting mobilization of world public opinion. It is known that in the Spanish Civil War, despite the proposals of the Non-Invervention Committee, the governments of Italy, Germany and the Soviet Union played decisive roles, and, in addition, there was a significant presence of the volunteers from all over the world who formed part of the famous International Brigades. The result of this internationalization of the Spanish War was the universalization of the conflict, converting our Civil War into a paradigm of all such wars or, if you will, it became a Universal Civil War.

Finally, there was no lack of an element characteristic of all nineteenth-century civil wars in the Spanish Civil War of 1936, that is, the telling intervention of the army, although this was accompanied by important variations, for in 1936 there was present a monolithic character representative of an indisputable national will. The army, which had polarized patriotism since the beginning of the century through the intermediacy of the Law of Jurisdictions of 1906, became the voice of national sovereignty, implacably snatching it from the people. This fact explains why they called the followers of General Franco "National Spain," while those faithful to the Republic and its government--democratically elected--were known as the "Popular Cause." They were also called "Reds," "Communists," or accursed representatives of "Anti-Spain," among other equally derogatory names. The "inquisitorial mentality," implicit in these epithets, gave rise to the conditions for the most important exile that ever occurred in a Spain where throughout centuries waves of exiles have been a commonplace thing.

The fondness for extermination which Franco's army harbored led their leader to decree, at the end of the war in 1939, that exile did not exist. When the computation of the number of war victims was made during the dictatorship, the historians of the regime always spoke of the "million dead," a figure which we know today to be clearly incorrect, but the psychological explanation could very well respond to the desire of the authorities in the Franco government to put the exiles in the list of the dead, since, from a civilian point of view, they were considered to be dead. It is a fact, of course, that high level authorities in the règime decreed that exile did not exist, except in the case of a small number of criminals and undesirables, and on account of this they created an administrative machinery to demonstrate their non-existence. It is frequent, in this sense, to hear speak of press censorship, but one unjustly forgets that censorship was only one of the mechanisms of concealment used by the government administrators. Among other means of censorship we find the following: customs control of publications, inspection of bookstores, expurgation of libraries, home searches, lawsuits against those who distributed publications considered to be clandestine, and so forth. The immediate historiographical result of such a policy was an impressive development of the bibliography of the Civil War--although it was only from the unilateral point of view of the victors--, and the almost complete absence of a bibliography on exile.

When in the 60's--once the inquisitorial vigilance was relatively relaxed--, some young writers, including myself, tried to scratch the wall of silence of the "non-existent Spain"--the word "exile" still could not be used--and so Marra-López had to use as the title of his book on exiled novelists *Spanish Narrative Outside of Spain* (1977). The death of General Franco and the change in politico-cultural circumstances made possible the extensive research undertaken by a large group of investigators, whose research produced the book *The Spanish Exile of 1939* (6 volumes, 1976-78), perhaps the most ambitious general book on the subject written until then. This work allowed us to visualize an immense territory as well as to detect its most salient characteristics, in this way enabling us to encompass the phenomenon about which much research remains to be done.

This is not the time to make a summary of what we could call the "state of the question," but rather to call attention to some of the central conclusions to which our study has led us. The first and most important conclusion is the exceptional consideration of the phenomenon. Although the exile of '39 may be considered the culmination of a Spanish history of exiles in the contemporary period, the circumstances surrounding it and its magnitude change it to take on the semblance of a unique phenomenon. "Never in the history of Spain had there been an exodus of this kind," says Vicente Lloréns.[1] Juan Marichal confirms this in a recent article in which he states that "the exile of 1939 was an entirely new phenomenon in the history of

Spain."[2] This unique character of the phenomenon made Marichal prophesy that it will not be repeated, which in our judgment, is in turn a consequence of the two phenomena which, for us, constitute an indissoluble unity: civil war and exile. These phenomena are the dramatic expression of the breakdown of the ability of the inhabitants of a nation to live together, which the "inquisitorial mentality" prevented. The civil war and subsequent diasporas caused a definitive crisis in our history of exiles and demonstrates the urgent necessity to adopt democracy and its democratic institutions in a civil living together at a time when there is a break with the isolationist schemes of the dominating national body in the last centuries.

Despite what we have written above, we must not forget what at first sight may appear to be a contradiction: the insertion of the Spanish exile of 1939 within the great migratory movements of Europe that had their origin in the political cataclysms of the twentieth century: the two World Wars, the Soviet Revolution and three totalitarian dictatorships. If the intervention of the German and Italian armies, as well as Soviet aid, manifested Spain's impossibility to attain an autarchic and isolationist policy, a parallel occurrence was confirmed with respect to exile, in the light of which it becomes evident that the exodus of the Spanish Republicans cannot be set apart from that of the Italian liberals, the German Jews, the White Russians or the Soviet Mensheviks. It is precisely on the strength of these occurrences that the paradigmatic character of the Spanish Civil War can be recognized as a Universal Civil War. The conclusion of this became evident to the most clear-sighted European minds: that Europe cannot survive with conflicting and clashing national policies, and for that reason there comes to the forefront the necessity to establish the political, social, economic and cultural bases of a united continent. The plan of a European Community as an unrenounceable program for a possible and hopeful future arises, which the Spanish exile of 1939 did not fail to include in its agenda. Let us remember that if the participation of Republican Spaniards was important in the French Resistance against the Nazis, as this is a matter that should not be separately viewed from the meeting called by the Congress of the European Movement which took place in Munich in 1962, and in which Spanish participants, both from the exile and from within Spain, made a vehement declaration of having Spain work in unison with the rest of Europe.

One fact closely linked to World War II is that a sizable percentage of Spanish exiles emigrated to America. As is well known, April 1, 1939, was the date given for the official end of the Spanish war, but in September of the same year the hostilities of World War II began. This circumstance, together with the welcome extended to the Spanish exiles by the Mexican government of Lázaro Cárdenas, led to a group of exiled Republicans taking up residence in Mexico. The number of these exiles ranged between 15,000 and 20,000.

Many other countries, Argentina, Chile and Venezuela, among others, aided in the generous reception accorded the refugees of the Civil War, although none of them equalled the exceptional generosity of Mexico, which became the seat of the Government of the Spanish Republic in Exile.

This fact was of extraordinary importance since it constituted the first massive emigration to those countries since dating back from the outset their political emancipation in 1824 in which were involved very large groups of Spaniards of high intellectual caliber. Throughout the nineteenth century the Spaniards who came to the American continent belonged to what we may call economic emigration: people of low social status and possessing no economic resources who would try to earn a living while starting from scratch in the countries to which they went. This was the army of those they called *gallegos* in Argentina and *gachupines* in Mexico. [Translator's note: these two words, used to describe Spaniards, have a pejorative meaning.] The exiles of 1939 did not conform to this pattern since a majority of them were highly endowed professionals and intellectuals. These émigrés not only altered the traditional image of Spain in the countries that welcomed them, but they themselves also underwent the impact of a new reality through their entering into a completely new experience that encompassed real contact with a world they only knew indirectly through readings, studies, friendships, etc. Most of them were to perform what they called a "new discovery of America," and through this was forged a "new image of Spain." In general, they all would become aware of the "unity of culture among the Spanish-speaking peoples."[3] See José Luis Abellán.

This awareness is at the heart of what constitutes a new existential situation, which some sought to express with new words. Of course, no one felt himself "banished from his land" and thus neologisms were used to describe the new situations. José Gaos used the word *transterrados* ("transplanted" or "relocated"). He explains it as follows:

> We did not feel ourselves 'exiled' but simply 'transplanted.' We Spaniards made a new discovery of America. We knew about Spanish America but how different that is from living its vastness and diversity in the present, its profundity and complexity in the past and a young people undergoing the process of fermentation. On account of these three things there is a plethora of possibilities for the future. But we had already initiated in Spain the activity that I am dealing with. It is that the recovery of Spanish values had begun in Spain, activated by the awareness of its merits. The purpose of this awareness translated itself in part in our being unable to foresee a life preferable to the one we had led and the possibility of our putting it behind us; at the time we had no inkling as to this possibility becoming a fact as it eventually came to pass, ushered in by violence. Fortunately, that which is Spanish in this America has allowed us to reconcile and recoup Spanish values and to testify to the fidelity proffered to them by the Americans.[4]

Juan Ramón Jiménez preferred to say that he felt himself *conterrado* [i.e. he felt at home in a land with people of similar heritage.]

> The miracle of my Spanish took place in the Argentine Republic . . . When we arrived at the port of Buenos Aires and I heard a group of children shout my name Juan Ramón! Juan Ramón! I felt myself a Spaniard, a reborn, revived Spaniard who came out of the land of exile, exhumed, with the stone of my Fuentepiña in my breast

pocket. The shout, the Spanish language, the shout in the Spanish language, the shout! And so Andalusian, which is to me the most authentically Spanish of Spain, eight centuries of Oriental culture, Andalusia . . . that very night I was speaking Spanish with my whole body and soul . . . and with my mother's language, the mutual smile, the embrace, the effusion. People moved around there like in Andalusia. It was the assurance of a conviction, a recognition which will be prolonged in this American existence of mine while I live. I am not a man without a tongue now nor an exile but a *conterrado* and because of having regained my tongue, I have found God in the awareness of the beautiful, which would have been impossible if I did not hear people speaking in Spanish. . . . [5]

From these experiences, there arises a new literature which is the product of the American impact. The old theme of Latin American dictatorship is renewed with works such as those of Francisco Ayala: *Muertes de perro* (*Dog Deaths*, 1959) and *Fondo del vaso* (*The Bottom of the Glass*, 1962) are perhaps the most significant. Spanish novelists are not immune to the magical realism of a reality founded on mystery, and so there comes into being those novels of Ramón J. Sender which deal with America: *Epitalamio del prieto Trinidad (Epithalamium of Black Trinidad,* 1942) and *La aventura equinocial de Lope de Aguirre (The Equinoctial Adventure of Lope de Aguirre,* 1945). In some cases it becomes evident that literature is going to constitute a channel for a new awareness of cultural encounter, expressed through a "literary symbiosis" as that which Manuel Andújar reflects in *Partiendo de la angustia (Departing from the Anguish, 1944).*[6]

The recovery of the cultural legacy of the exile of '39 in which we are involved, is slowly demonstrating that Spanish culture of the twentieth century constitutes a planetary culture of incalculable consequences. This is what Juan Marichal expressed some time ago: "the culture of the Spanish language is one of the few really 'planetary' cultures of the modern world."[7]

It is clear to us today that the recovery of Spanish culture can only be done if we resume the connection which many literary historians as a rule call the Age of Silver (1885-1935), but that connection will be impossible if we do not recoup the cultural legacy of the exile represented by the names of Pablo Picasso, Juan Ramón Jiménez, José Ortega y Gasset, Luis Buñuel, F. García Lorca, Antonio Machado, Severo Ochoa, Jorge Guillén and the endless number of creators, thinkers and artists who were driven to exile in 1939. Only when we have done this--that is to say, when that legacy has been fully restored--will we be at the historical level which Spain has made herself worthy of as attested by her enormous intellectual effort, which some renowned Spaniards have attained during the twentieth century. What these eminent Spaniards have achieved has not been sufficiently recognized due to the distortions the Civil War and an exile drawn out over more than 40 years have exerted on our cultural reality, traumatizing numerous personal biographies, twisting the messages of our creators and making difficult the diffusion of their work.

This year [1989] marks the fiftieth anniversary of that dramatic event and the situation is not negative. Besides the global vision of the phenomenon and its importance, mentioned above, we know that there are diverse groups of investigators working on different areas of exile. Some regional works have been initiated as those which have already begun to be provided in Mexico,[8] and in Argentina[9] if this spreads, it is likely that the forgotten terrain which we began to plough many years ago will become a garden. But of greater importance are the philosophical reflections of some exiles who upon already seeing the physical cycle of the exile over, with the restoration of democracy in Spain, are beginning to realize that exile forms a part of the human condition. In 1977 the philosopher Adolfo Sánchez Vázquez, wrote the epilogue to a collective volume of short stories on exile which had the following significant title: "End of Exile and Exile Without End." At that juncture of his life, the exiled philosopher realized that he could return to his country, but that his return, if it took place, would cause as strong a spiritual anguish as the one that he felt on leaving his country after the Civil War. Roots had sprouted in the country of refuge and to leave his new country would be as painful as it had been for him to stay there for so many years. Therefore, to remain in the country that so generously put out the welcome mat, "far from smoothing over the contradiction which causes anguish in the exiled person, increases it more and more. Before, the exile only took into account what was lost on departing from his country; now one must take into account what one stands to lose upon leaving behind the country in which one has settled. This is a dramatic piece of bookkeeping." The decision is impossible, since he who is in this situation finds himself facing an unsolvable alternative, for he is torn between two loyalties. Sánchez Vázquez says:

> And then the exile discovers, first with amazement, then with sorrow, later with a certain irony, at the very moment in which he objectively has ended his exile, that time has not passed with impunity and that, whether he returns or not, he will never stop being an exile. He may return, but a new nostalgia and a new idealization will take hold of him. He may remain, but never will he be able to renounce the past which brought him here, and now bereft of the future that he dreamed of for so many years. At the end of the long journey of exile, being torn more than ever, the exile sees himself condemned to be an exile forever. But the dramatic bookkeeping that he sees himself forced to keep does not unavoidably have to function only with some ciphers. He will be able to carry his accounting with a sum of losses, of disillusions and hopelessnesses, but his accounting can also be based on a sum of two roots, of two lands, of two hopes. The decisive thing is to be loyal, here or there, to that which caused a person to be cast into exile. The decisive thing is not to be in a certain place but how an exile is faring.[10]

Here is a beautiful lesson of adherence to destiny, acted out by María Zambrano, after her return to Spain. In response to my recent request of this illustrious thinker to send me a text to inaugurate a course on exile that I conducted at El Escorial during the summer of 1989, she wrote:

> There are certain journeys that are understood only after the traveler returns. For me, from that examination made on my return, the exile that I have lived is essential. I do not conceive of my life without the exile I have lived. Once exile is experienced it is unrenounceable. I make this confession, because to speak of certain topics is

senseless if the truth is not said; I confess that it has taken a lot of work to renounce my forty years of exile, a lot of work. Despite the generosity that Madrid and all Spain have bestowed on me, and the love that I have found in so many people, from time to time it grieves me. It is a sensation akin to one who has been flayed to death, like Saint Bartholomew, an unintelligible sensation, but that is the way it is. I believe that exile is an essential dimension of human life, but on saying this, I burn my lips because I would not want anybody to experience exile again. Everybody should be considered as human beings and at the same time cosmic beings who should not know exile.[11]

Exile lived to its limit, experienced to its utmost human radical degree, as it affects Sánchez Vázquez and María Zambrano, becomes a philosophical category like other situations that have their limits: death, illness, jail, love, anguish. . . . From any of these, meditation on human life acquires characteristics of unusual depth and trancendence. I think that the poetic experience of Juan Ramón Jiménez is relevant to that experience of the exile. During his residence in Puerto Rico, his poetry achieved an authentic philosophic-religious dimension which has not been sufficiently probed and publicized. In reality, from his *Estación total (Total Season, 1946)* to *Dios deseado y deseante (God Desired and Desiring, 1959)*, his poetry undergoes a process of purification influenced by the experience exile afforded him.

It is precisely life in exile which provided him with a detachment from the accessory and the temporary until he arrived at a bareness which is called "pure poetry." He meant by this an "essential lyric" for which the only thing that counts is access to wholeness of beauty, understood in a Platonic sense, revealing its theological and metaphysical essence.

Recent studies have shown the importance that some philosophical influences had on Juan Ramón's attitude toward poetry: especially Spanish Krausism and theological modernism, but I believe that very few have understood in what sense, with the aid of such a resource, he was able to mould beauty from the fountainhead of exile he encountered in that Caribbean island.

. . . . .

It is a fact that Juan Ramón's poetry had gone through stages of distillation that led it to a symbolism that paved the way to the search of a "total season" in which the universe, purified of all that is secondary, acquires meaning. As one of the most sagacious critics says, "The poetic struggle of Juan Ramón contains a philosophical trajectory toward the possession of a truth which affirms itself as the poet attains aesthetic purity. In this hypostatis of truth and beauty the symbolic expression turns out to be decisive. The symbol comes to be the aesthetic crystallization of the truth with its halo of mystery and suggestions."[12]

From that point of view, the symbol for our poet becomes a "sacrament of beauty," in which the converging oppositions make sense. It does not surprise us then that Juan Ramón himself has defined poetry as "an attempt to attain the absolute by means of symbols."[13] Hence the previous critic extracts this pertinent conclusion: "If authentic literary modernism is, in the long run, symbolist modernism, this in turn becomes the vehicle through which he expresses his metaphysical and theological consciousness; particularly if, as we shall see, the symbolism comes to be, moreover, a fundamental characteristic of theological modernism."[14]

The different symbolic elements of this universe are fused holistically in the direction of monism; therefore, in the words of this author quoted above, "unity and plurality, calm and movement are not opposed in Juan Ramón." His monism is as dynamic as his symbolism. It is, however, a complex monism: a dialectic monism. God and the cosmos, universal consciousness and the consciousness of Juan Ramón, for example, become dialectically resolved in unity and totality. The being becomes unity in movement and the becoming is movement toward unity."[15]

From the semantic point of view, this symbolism is resolved in a polyhedral structure in which it is impossible to perceive all the meanings simultaneously, or thereupon to express them poetically, a fact that does not impede the hidden presence of the palpable whole to come forth making the consciousness of universal monism evident. The multiple symbolic contents, although not manifest, hint at their presence through the permanent evocation of the whole.

Beauty created or recreated in this way involves the poet "who passes from the one who dominates to being dominated. He is metamorphosed into a 'god' who defines him, the poet; or better still the work itself recreates the poet as it asserts him successively as creator. The active and the passive in continuous movement enter into a dialectic of constant indetermination in the manner of the theory that Heisenberg establishes for electronic physics. This is the dialectic of a 'god who is desired and is desiring'."[16]

In this sense we can affirm the existence of a "vital immanence" in Juan Ramón's vision of the cosmos which, given his mystic and deist background, has been called pantheism. Although the existence of a unity among god, world and beauty is evident in him, the omnipresence of his "I" never disappears; for that reason, a critic has written in a restricted sense: "We come to the conclusion that Juan Ramón's metaphysics of immanence is founded on the subjective unity of the tryptic I-universe-god, thus establishing, together with this threefold relationship, the axiomatic character of "I" as beginning and end. The whole system seems to tend to consolidate the immortality of the I; an I in which everything becomes mystically and naturally present, in which all is found and is resolved. If we looked for a term, we could perhaps call the system of Juan Ramón 'pan-I-ism': all is in the I and the I is everything. It is the subject of the poet in the act of creating which is verified by each word, which, while hardly pronounced, resides as a new being in his counsciousness. In this new being the I lives in an always renewed relationship with absolute immanence."[17]

Juan Ramón's pantheism seems to us deeply heterodox, understood in its traditional sense, and perhaps it should be termed panentheism. Nevertheless, his "god," as a permanent universal consciousness, permits us to inscribe him fully within a modernism that tries to fuse the theological and the aesthetic in an indissoluble unity.

The poet manages thus to overcome his situation as an exile, placing himself in a mystical experience of beauty which changes him into a universal man; in this sense has Juan Ramón Jiménez been called a "universal Andalusian," hailing from a habitat where there is room for all men. Once more, as was the case with other Spanish exiles, does the experience derived therefrom become a creative source of the most profound humanity.

NOTES

[1] "La emigración republicana de 1939," in *El exilio español de 1939* (Madrid: Taurus, 1976).

[2] Juan Marichal. "La singularidad histórica del exilio español," read in a course on the exile of 1939 at El Escorial, 28-31 of August, 1989.

[3] José Luis Abellán, "Filosofía y pensamiento: Su función en el exilio de 1939," in *El exilio español de 1939* (Madrid: Taurus, 1976), III, 151-208.

[4] "Los 'transterrados' españoles de la filosofía en México," in *Filosofía mexicana de nuestros días* (México: 1954), 313-16.

[5] *La corriente infinita* (México: Aguilar, 1947), 306-08.

[6] Manuel Andújar. "Narrativa del exilio español y literatura latinoamericana," in *Cuadernos Hispanoamericanos*, 295, January, 1975.

[7] Juan Marichal. "De algunas consecuencias intelectuales de la guerra civil española," in *El nuevo pensamiento político español* (México: Finisterre, 1966), 68.

[8] *El exilio español en México 1939-1982*, México: Fondo de Cultura Económica, 1982.

[9] Emilia de Zuleta, "El exilio español de 1939 en la Argentina," in *Boletín de Literatura Comparada*. Universidad Nacional de Cuyo, Mendoza, XI-XII, 1986-87.

[10] A. Sánchez Vázquez. "Fin del exilio y exilio sin fin," epilogue to the book of short story entitled *¡Exilio!*, México: 1977.

[11] The text was prepared by María Zambrano for the course on Spanish exile of 1939 given at El Escorial, 28-31 August, 1989.

[12] J.A. Reula Paul. "Algunas constantes del pensamiento español en Juan Ramón Jiménez." Doctoral thesis presented at Universidad de La Laguna (1986-87,), 187.

[13] Ricardo Gullón, *Conversaciones con Juan Ramón Jiménez* (Madrid: Taurus, 1958), 107.

[14] Reula Paul, loc. cit. p. 203.

[15] Ibid. 212.

[16] Ibid. 219.

[17] Ibid. 320.

[Translation of an unpublished essay requested by the editor.]

FRANCISCO AYALA

Francisco Ayala was born in Granada in 1906. He studied law and humanities at the University of Madrid where he received his doctorate in law. He won the competition to obtain the chair of political law at the Central University of Madrid. When the Republican party lost the Civil War (1936-39), he left Spain to reside in Buenos Aires where he remained until 1950. He taught at the University of Puerto Rico for a few years and in 1956 he went to live in the United States. He taught at several American universities; Rutgers, Bryn Mawr, New York University, Chicago and Brooklyn College (SUNY). He now resides in Madrid. Ayala is a novelist, short story writer, excellent sociologist, literary critic, and prolific essayist who has written on a large variety of topics dealing with Spanish and Latin American culture and history. His famous *Tratado de sociología (Treatise on Sociology)*, originally published in 1947 as a textbook, has gone through a number of editions. He has won several literary prizes, including the prestigious Cervantes Prize, the National Prize of Literature and the Prize of National Letters (1988).

THE RISE AND FALL OF MODERNITY

The issue of modernity has given rise to a good deal of rhetoric and many vain discussions, and one fears that this may continue beyond 1992, the year that commemorates the Fifth Centenary of the Discovery of America. Why then amid such abundant prose can't I voice some of my own reflections about the meaning attributable to the events that took place in the year in which the ships of the Spanish expedition set anchor at that port which for Europeans would become a New World for the Europeans?

It is a well-known fact that historical chronology has a conventional value, which is undoubtedly useful but conventional nevertheless. While the chronology has not as yet been revoked and replaced, although attempts to alter it have surfaced, we accept the current periodicity which establishes that the modern epoch dates from the Renaissance. So much is made today of postmodernity, a so-called contemporary period that has been proposed without much success, that it seems appropriate to ask ourselves what the parameters of that modernity can be now considered ended.

For me--and I will tell why later--the modern epoch opens with the expeditions of discovery, conquest and colonization symbolized by what Columbus accomplished in 1492, and closes with the spectacular but unproductive and sterile voyage to the moon which we witnessed on television in 1969. It is worthwhile to note parenthetically something which would be obvious: from a human point of view, as far as a feat of heroic bravery is concerned, Columbus' undertaking was, above all comparisons, much more risky and demanded much greater bravery than the recent feat, since those who accomplished it, set out, toward the completely unknown without having contact with their base. But this is beside the point. In both cases, the expeditionary forces were agents of Western Christian civilization which during the whole course of modernity had maintained the historical initiative, and from whose perspective the concept of universal history was to be generated. This concept implies a totalizing vision of the action of men on earth, corresponding to a historical development which would integrate the variable world into a technologically closed planetary unity.

In truth, one could also take as a point of initial reference the date in which, thirty years after Columbus' voyage, the expedition of Magellan-Elcano would accomplish the circling of the globe, creating in our Western man the clear and definitive awareness of inhabiting a limited sphere which can be circled and can be completely explored and dominated in its entirety. Navigational knowledge and skill, which at that time made possible such enterprises, were acquired from the Renaissance stimulus of scientific curiosity and the military expansion which revolutionized, the art of war already during the reign of the Catholic Monarchs. At the same time, it was indispensable to revolutionize the economic and political power in a bureaucratic organization that would give rise to a national state. The history of science informs us how the passage from theoretical knowledge to its practical application--that is, technology--has been linked basically to designs dealing with the waging of wars. The title of engineer originally referred to the military profession.

With the establishment of absolute monarchies, the development of the modern age describes the process of European man's virtual conquest of the earth's totality and the incorporation of diverse peoples to his own culture. What does not fail to astonish us is that this task has been able to be accomplished, as has been the case during four centuries, not through the work of Christianity as a block but through the separate initiative of several national states. Moreover, these states have been locked in a stiff reciprocal competition which by nature was always very violent armed confrontation. In the struggle of these rivalries certain game rules were respected--or rules of war--while territories abroad remained vacant and available for exploitation. World War I (1914-18) doubtlessly marks the end of this situation and the end of the modern age. World War II (1939-45) definitively introduced among European nations the concept of a total war which does not seek the mere defeat of the adversary but his complete annihilation.

The arsenal applied to such a purpose already had had a terrifying efficiency as a result of the continual technological progress. At the end of this last great war, the first atomic bombs made all too evident their potential capacity to destroy the human race and perhaps to pulverize or cause the disappearance of the world it inhabits. This technological progress, in implements of war as in other fields, had made ridiculously small the power structures of sovereign national states, and demanded now an organization provided with global authority since the instruments of current civilization had annulled the distances of space and time. There were no exempt territories nor more countries to discover, explore or colonize, and the world had been changed into a unity enclosed in a network, filled more and more with media of communication and control.

The 1969 expedition to the moon is at the same time the result of the incomparable impulse of the Conquistadors which motivated European man since the Renaissance and offers a pathetic proof of his futility. This is an impulse which, because of its own success, has lost purpose and been exhausted, and consequently thought to be limited to the fantasy of games, if not to the delirium of space voyages or to equally fantastic galactic wars.

I understand that this newly created situation serves to explain the most gaudy phenomena of this postmodernity in which we find ourselves. During the multisecular historical period that unfolded with the naval expeditions which the date of the Discovery of America symbolizes and ended with World War II--or perhaps with the conquest of the moon in 1969--Christianity extended its power until it covered the entire planet, encompassing all of earth's inhabitants in a material civilization that is ever more advanced, more effective, more dominating. And even now, when the resourses of that civilization have become incalculable, those formidable energies deployed in the process have been devoid of a goal: contemporary man has the world in his hands but he does not know what application to make of the fabulous technology which he has developed, he does not know how to use it, he does not know what to make of his life. Thus, having become disoriented and uncertain in general, the world argues about the continuous outbreaks of an ubiquitous violence, which has become more devasting since the means offered by high technology to carry it out are now available to anybody. It is a violence scarcely hidden at times under the cloak of tenuous and residual ideological pretexts, but more often deprived of the slightest pretense of justification and, alternatively, the fall into the stagnation of indolence or suicide from drugs. Who could be capable of predicting whether this situation will lead to the final catastrophe or if, on the contrary, humanity will find the way to transcend it on the path toward a happier stage.

TO ENLIGHTEN PUBLIC OPINION

Television is frequently accused of falsifying and vilifying the political process by presenting to the viewer's eye not the substance of matters of common interest but the image projected by public men entrusted with the management of the public welfare. This reproach is unjustified in my opinion. It seems to me that that approach through television of the figure, facial expressions, gestures and words of the managers of the public welfare restores democracy to its pristine originality and even permits the expansion and deepening of popular government to limits formerly inconceivable. Let us not forget that direct democracy, as it was practiced in the Greek *polis* and until recently has been practiced in small communities all over Europe, functioned through the contact between candidates or public officials and the assembly of its fellow citizens, who were personally acquainted with each other. These public officials whom they saw and listened to in the flesh, with whom they may have had discussions and, in any event, in whom they placed their confidence, and, from whom they withdrew it if they later for some reason had a mind to do so. These links of close relationship were still maintained in representative democracy by the election of deputies in small electoral districts, while in the populated urban centers and ultimately in the electoral systems the purpose of which are to orchestrate a democracy of masses, it became increasingly apparent that there had come about an inevitable distance between those who seek public posts and the anonymous people called upon to decide with their ballots.

It will be said that in this way, putting personal preferences aside, that only ideas and legislative or governmental programs will gain consideration. But we all know that this does not go beyond being a good-hearted desire spawned from optimistic rationalism and that nobody is unaware of the fact that the name of the person who is more or less known and who figures at the top of a list will be the one to win over the voters with his supposed charisma. (We will shortly return to this matter of charisma.) No matter how the programs or ideological orientations can weigh upon the minds of people, such elements appear embodied in concrete persons, and given that the human factor turns out to be predominant, not to say decisive, something that perhaps is disastrous in its results, but nonetheless in the last analysis, is positive, and in any case, inescapable. The political relationship is ultimately one of confidence, no matter how much that confidence may seem to be shattered or on occasions maliciously betrayed. Demogogues have always been adept at maliciously betraying the confidence of people, and demagogues were the first to discover during our century how to manipulate that confidence in order to take full advantage so as to promote their own purposes through the enormous possiblities of mass communication. The period between the two wars offered the pathetic and terrifying contrast between arthritic democracies confined to their traditional institutions and those prodigious madmen, a Mussolini, a Hitler, who put into play all the technical resources within their reach to mobilize the multitudes and enchant them with their charisma (a concept coined by Max Weber and which today, though applied to any imitator of much lesser talent than they possessed, still appropriately singles out the ones previously mentioned as those who reaped full benefit from the practice of its use). The secret of that charisma, its sad attractiveness, consisted of the capacity to establish contact with the multitudes, calling on them to participate in an historical destiny. Very different from this issue is that this call would find expression in manipulation and end up in deceitful and perverse destiny.

World War II brought an end to those prodigous madmen, and democracy again prevailed in the West. But during the almost half century that has passed since its end, and while the technology of communication has developed with record-breaking speed, this technology, called "mass media," is insufficiently and clumsily utilized in the political game of democratic governments. There are several causes for such a deficiency. In my judgment, the main one is that in the new phase of universal history since the end of World War II, the governmental institutions which present-day society requires, have not been set up. Our society is one of masses, poorly served by those institutions which had functioned very adequately in the sovereign nation of the bourgeois epoch, when the Parliament was a theater in which, with efficient drama, public opinion was formed and authoritative decisions were made. Now the center of such decisions has been transferred to the super powers. At the same time--in large measure due to the technological revolution, with its economic consequences--the population has become homologized and unified internationally.

In this new society of masses, the great political sounding board that Parliament was has lost its position to the audio-visual media, principally to television. From the parliamentary sessions, as is the case of any other political act, only what the television cameras capture and transmit gets across to society. Through the home screen is brought into play the contact between the current or potential public affairs representatives and the people whose votes will decide who should occupy official posts. This being the case, it is not surprising that those who aspire to win or continue to be incumbents of these posts fiercely compete in gaining access to the medium of radio and especially to television. This, as I said at the beginning, seems good to me, but there is no doubt that however much one speculates on image manipulation, what is certain is that, before the implacable eye of the camera, the human quality of the subject, when subjected to scrutiny, reveals much more than the human quality of the politician shaking hands and kissing children in his publicity campaign. Everybody realized that the electoral triumph of President Kennedy over Nixon in the United States was due to their debates on television, or rather, to the contrast of their respective personalities revealed to the viewers. People have blamed television for the large number of votes Reagan obtained, forgetting the inanity of the candidates offered to the public, and forgetting also the enormous abstention of votes at the polls.

No, the blame can not be placed on the medium or the instrument but on those who use it poorly. My many years of experience as observer of the North American political scene persuade me that the use of television made in that country has almost always been poor since it has been exploited merely as a propaganda vehicle in its crudest sense, even using publicity spots produced with the same technique--and by the same technicians--as commercials. The characteristics of an isolationist democracy, which felt itself self-sufficient and very powerful, permitted the cruel and heartless political struggle to adhere to private interests, making it its business to avoid going to the heart of the great problems. I think that this may explain such a perversion.

On the other hand, I do not know the exact contents of Soviet television, but I have the impression that until now it has scarcely been utilized there in the political game despite being the monopoly of an authoritarian regime. It may be that the extreme conservatism of that regime, its never-say-die hard-core paralysis, would make it fearful of the dangers inherent in so dynamic a medium.

All of this seems to have begun to change now. In a recent editorial *El País* [popular Spanish daily newspaper] made a fine analysis of the spectacle offered by television to the entire world in presenting the ceremonies dealing with the disarmament treaty signed in Washington, and pointed out the novelty of the situation, detecting in it the possible prelude to other sensational news, announced perhaps in a similar manner. Should I dare to venture my opinion on the reasons underlying the change that may occur?

During the last four decades the planet has lived under the control of two rival superpowers. The changes that have been made, about which its rulers have not taken due notice, have had their effects which are now unavoidable. On the one hand, the senseless, really absurd, arms race to which their rivalry has driven them, has brought both of them to the point of crushing each other's colossal and imperial might. The arms race has impeded Soviet economic development in the direction of its social welfare, and by mortgaging its economy the United States has come face to face with a frightful budget deficit. In the meantime, while Europe has not been able to organize itself so as to hammer out a political unity that would speak with a voice of its own, the economic growth within its communities garners effective autonomy opposite a United States in the throes of experiencing the need of seeking help from its former subordinates with a view to getting out of difficult straits. And to seek help also from Japan, whose fabulous development, with the perspective of a congruent rapid industrialization of the Asiatic continent, places Western hegemony in doubt.

This means that the world order designed in Yalta, on whose pillars the life of the planet has developed, is bankrupt and needs a reappraisal, at the very least, some readjustment. The frightening useless production of weapons by the two superpowers is crushing them, while in their respective spheres of domination or influence, new powers with prudent attitudes are beginning to emerge. An industrialized Asiatic continent will reduce the West to very modest dimensions, notwithstanding the weight of its present-day assets, especially when the means to develop the remaining potential for industrialization of the whole American continent are not forthcoming. And Europe--Europe in its entirety on both sides of the Iron Curtain--while beseiged by the disturbing fringe of Islamic countries which have not been able to assume modernity through adaptation to it, and which, reacting to domestic maltreatment and offense, have relapsed into a desperate fundamentalism which is destructive and self-destructive.

A catalogue of errors would be interminable if we were to list all the errors committed by these two self-centered great powers, errors which have engaged them in a blind struggle over decades, and now they both feel their power cracking. Underneath each one of the many lamentable episodes which fill recent history one finds the basic error of having wanted to govern the world without an effective communication with the governed, without associating the multitudes with the problems of the government, this being in actuality the basic concern of democracy. Instead of posing and discussing the real issues in the field of publicity, efforts have been made to intoxicate the people with stupid clichés. Thus, for example, to claim that the United States carried forth its poorly planned geopolitical movements with the purpose of defending human freedom or rights against the evil empire, or that the Soviet Union sent its forces to free oppressed people by bringing socialism to them, was a mockery only to be believed by those who wanted to be deceived. And such messages were transmitted by the centers of world power through the media of communication to a humanity submerged in the difficulties of adapting itself to those new forms of coexistence which advanced technology imposes. It is not surprising then that the unbridled and forsaken masses should be caught up in universal confusion.

Let us hope that the opening--or overture--of the television spectacle offered to the world on the occasion of a disarmament treaty may be the prelude to a positive historical phase that is headed toward the integration of a more reasonable world order in which the democracy of the masses is articulated through the resources of electronic communication, so that an enlightened public opinion may effectively participate in the government of society.

LANGUAGE, LITERATURE AND POLITICS

I have always tried to assert the autonomy of artistic creation in general, and literary creation in particular, as well as the work of art itself, even as I frequently accept the fact that other fields of activity can be more pressing and of greater importance. But at the same time that I asserted the autonomy of art, I have tried to recognize that the interference and influence of other factors on literature, especially that of politics, in its conditioning as in its social effectiveness, and above all in the latter. A single fact to which I have alluded several times in the past is that any kind of hogwash published in English is immediately translated into all languages while the brilliant work of a Portuguese or Lithuanian poet may be published in translation by chance, if it ever does appear, clearly illustrates what I mean. The relationship between political power and literary prestige constitutes an unavoidable reality, not always so gross as in the example I have called forth, since it manifests itself in very diverse forms and at times in too subtle a form, though it does constitute a reality we have to reckon with, by which is meant that we could ourselves be dragged along or confused by it. Our judgments and opinions must be put on a conceptually clear basis.

Several years ago I proposed a kind of axiom which others have picked up and repeated: that the writers' country is his language. And as far back as 1952 I published an essay in which, under the title of "The Writer of the Spanish Language," I tried to justify this assertion, founded on the cultural community that the language incorporates. "Why," I asked myself, "is it necessary to affirm the obvious since all writers in my language constitute a unique literature, a single body of culture?" And I answered myself: "Because, with our country's decline in historical initiative and their political division in several states, which I do not consider at all as an evil but perhaps an invaluable good, we have become entangled in inappropriate fallacies of nationalism to the exaggerated point of postulating national literatures which have no other reality than that of ideological affirmation, an aspiration dictated by considerations or feelings of a political nature and completely alien from literature. Thus, it has not occurred to anybody to eliminate from French letters the name of J.J. Rousseau, so as to group him with Gottfried Keller in a presumed Swiss literature. Keller being a Swiss, and Hoffmansthal, an Austrian, have their place along with Rilke, born in Bohemia, in German literature. While each Belgian writer of the Walloon branch would be offended with one who would want to exclude him from

French literature, we constantly hear talk of Ecuadorean, Panamanian, Cuban, Argentine, Chilean literature, etc., or the advocacy, when this seems too absurd, of a literary nationalism that extends throughout Latin America and is separate from the literature of Spain. And the fact is that real local traits are not scarce in the literary production of all those countries--how could they be?--although, to be truthful, they are too tenuous and almost exclusively reduced to thematic material, and the picturesqueness they have in common seems to stem from their not knowing where they stand or from a sense of rootlessness. But even in the aspect in which such external traits touch the nerve of literature, as occurs with the use of *local* language, this only serves to confirm the presence of a simple nuance in the literary unity of the language."

These words were written when the consequences of the Spanish Civil War had made literary relations problematic within the scope of the Spanish language. The triumphant régime was instrumental in the isolation of a sector of Spanish intellectuals and in having expelled from Spain other sectors, made up of considerable numbers, that were to scatter chiefly throughout Spanish-speaking America. The protracted exile of these intellectuals led me to pose first in my own mind and then publicly in 1948, the question "for whom are we writing?" The ideology and practice of the Franco régime, with its stale historical traditionalism, had to awaken reactions of antipathy on the American continent. I have no doubt that its false claims of hegemony, even when reduced to the innocuousness of mere rhetoric, had to accentuate the positions of that cultural nationalism, which in Spanish American countries had become a definite anti-Spanish tradition, equal to what was called anti-Spain in the Peninsula. The verbiage spent over "the language of the Empire" could not fail to stir up antagonism in those countries, even when in the face of Spain's inanity amid the powers of the post-World War II world this antagonism had managed to take on so grotesque an image. But, if outside of the boundaries of Spain the policy inspired in such ideas was practically insignificant, within Spain, on the other hand, it turned out to be too effective. It was converted into an instrument of power, and the Spanish language was used to oppress and repress other languages of the Peninsula. It is not surprising that those people affected most, mainly the Catalans, were largely used as political instruments in the struggle against the régime.

From those post-World War II years to this day circumstances have changed a lot, and have been changing during a process in which I believe it is indispensable to highlight several outstanding points: the somewhat ingenuous confusion that peninsular writers experienced in discovering the literary creativity produced in our common language outside the Spanish state during the cultural black-out of the Franco régime; the world-wide boom achieved by the Spanish-American novel; and the exile suffered by many writers from that continent at the time when the pressure exerted by the dictatorship began to weaken.

Now we are finally installed in democracy and the positions have been inverted to a large degree. With regard to the basic literary community founded on the Spanish language, this republic of letters of which all of us who write in Spanish are citizens regardless of the civil citizenship of each one of us, it seems to me that no appreciable discrepancies exist. There will be somebody who will try to trace the origins of Guatemalan literature to the Mayas, or the origin of Andalusian literature to the Arabs, but those fantasies reveal too much the inevitable intrusion of political factors or nationalistic ideology in the field of poetic creation. Such intrusion is the source of very disturbing confusion. The nationalistic ideology formulated by German romanticism at the beginning of the 19th century concisely captured the most genuine expression of the national spirit, and each nation laid claim to being an independent and sovereign state. But the relationship between a nation and its language is very uncertain, very variable, as one approaches the field of practice. The state has used the language as an instrument of national unification--think of the *langue d'oil* in France or Castilian in the case of Spain--just as the rising nationalistic movements support the local language to substantiate their political claims. We have abundant examples of both things.

And if we look at the matter from the angle of literature, the lack of a clear and adequate conceptual distinction between the writer's country (his language) and that of the citizen (the state of which each one is a subject) causes various vacillations, perplexities and incongruencies, which must make us reflect. It is not easy at all. Look at what happens to the adjective *español* (Spanish) when we have to apply it to literary matters. For those writers who are citizens of Spanish American countries, it is embarrassing to use the label "Spanish" to affirm, which frequently happens here in Spain, that Catalan, Galician or Basque literatures or languages are Spanish, which is to attribute to the State the ultimate and definitive criterion in a matter that does not concern it. We are facing, of course, a problem of conceptualism, a very serious problem. I remember only too well that when Angel del Río published in the United States his excellent anthology, *History of Spanish Literature*, I had a friendly conversation with him regarding the fact that that admirable book excludes writers in the Spanish language born in America (except in the case of Rubén Darío, whose supreme influence makes his inclusion indispensable), but, on the other hand, he dedicates separate sections to the Catalan and Galician literatures which, in my opinion, insulted the dignity of these illustrious literatures, which were relegated to a secondary category. Evidently the criterion with which the book had been conceived was that of inserting the poetic creation within the framework of a determined political State.

This is the criterion that now seems to prevail among us. The policy of linguistic oppression established upon the exclusivity of Castilian [i.e., the major language of Spain] has been replaced by a policy of acceptance, recognition and official promotion of other peninsular languages. And although this is a conceptual matter, it is not merely so from the point of view of mere semantics, since it is charged with practical consequences in which the ambiguity is very visible. Thus, for example, there are highly endowed literary prizes in Spain open to all writers in the Spanish language (i.e. Castilian). But if Catalan, Galician or Basque are also Spanish languages since there are writers in today's Spanish state who write in these languages, why are their works excluded from these contests? We all know that what is involved is not just an abstract, theoretical issue. And we can all glimpse the political ingredients which it contains. Because inevitably, as I said at the beginning, literary creativity is always shaded to some degree by the political conditioning of one or another tendency, and its social effectiveness is subjected to similar factors. The German language and its literature served as an instrument, at the beginning of the past century, to arouse in the central European countries where German was spoken, as a nationalistic agglutination against the Napoleonic Empire. The French and Spanish languages were an instrument of national unification in the countries in which they were spoken. The languages spoken in several regions of the planet have been and are still utilized as instruments of nationalistic promotions and these are only some of the manifestations of great influence to which many others could be added. In the efforts to mobilize power, the most diverse social activities for this purpose are brought into play. Politics invade the field of letters and influence literature in different ways. It would not be worthwhile to lament something which cannot be remedied.

We suffer from a lot of confusion here in Spain at this time of change [from a dictatorship to democracy] when, instead of persecuting and oppressing peninsular languages which are different from Castilian, as the previous régime did, the public authorities recognize and respect them. This new policy, which I believe to be a proper one, has given way to attitudes of paternalistic encouragement and even to revengeful pressures. Not long ago I had to express my solidarity with the complaint of a Galician writer whom several of his countrymen zealously reproached for writing in Castilian, and I suspect that some prominent Galician writers would find intolerable for nationalistic reasons the notion that Galician forms part of the Portuguese language. We are witnessing an analogous situation in Valencia, where many resist accepting the fact that their own language belongs to the linguistic area of Catalan. It is undeniable that political reason prevails there over historical and cultural realities.

[These three essays are from Ayala's book *Mi cuarto a espadas (My Point of View,* 1988]

ELIAS DIAZ

Elías Díaz was born in 1934 in Salamanca. He received a law degree at the University of Salamanca where he taught as adjunct professor for a couple of years. He studied in Italy where he obtained a doctorate in law at the University of Bologna. In 1974 he won the competition to attain the chair of Philosophy of Law at the University of Oviedo and three years later he obtained the chair in this field at the Autonomous University of Madrid. He has taught and lectured at almost every university in Spain and also at quite a few universities in Italy, the United States (Duke, Pittsburgh, New York University), England, Puerto Rico, Mexico, Argentina, Brazil and Chile. He has written numerous books and articles on law, sociology and the intellectual history of Spain. His best-known book was published under the titles *Notas para una historia del pensamiento español actual (1939-1973) (Notes for a History of Recent Spanish Thought)* [1974] and *Pensamiento español en la era de Franco (1939-1975) (Spanish Thought in the Franco Era)* [1983]. This work which deals with the intellectual history of twentieth-century Spain, has passed through several editions.

THE NEW SOCIAL PACT: POLITICAL INSTITUTIONS AND SOCIAL MOVEMENTS

When one speaks today of the crisis of legitimacy of the State and of Law, one is fundamentally alluding to the problems that result from the lack of support for the social state or the welfare state characteristic of our time. I would like to begin my discussion of this with two preliminary but basic observations. The first one refers to the crisis of the welfare state. In my opinion, there is no reason for this crisis to drag down all the elements that characterize the worthwhile advances made by the social state, a fact which hypothetically would entail a loss of viability. These elements are not homogeneous but dual and at times even contradictory. In my understanding, breaking out of the crisis should not mean, as is the case today, that we follow the path of restrictive neoconservatism but rather that we undertake a profound study and democratic authentication of the social state. A second observation would emphasize that this crisis is not only that of an economic model of accumulation but also a crisis of legitimacy, that is to say of cultural and social values, of a "conception of the world" within which there is a significant philosophical debate (analytical, dialectical, postmodernist, etc.). My proposal of a new and necessary social contract attempts to provide a way to solve the problem of illegitimacy and to set forth a "legitimate legitimacy" of the present-day state and law based on more solid social and cultural foundations.

The "old paradigm" as Claus Offe puts it,[1] has had broad acceptance for its efficacious updatedness until the crisis of 1973 which had already begun in the sixties. Until that time and since the very end of World War II, the model, for better or worse, has functioned with its peculiar dualistic meaning. Those were possibly the best moments of the welfare state and of the social state.[2] It would not be fair, despite everything, that because of the current regressive movement toward conservative neoliberalism, the rehabilitation of the social state would make one forget the contemporary criticisms which, without denying its positive aspects, had been directed against it from the dyed-in-the-wood left, from Communists and libertarians, and most particularly from social democrats.[3]

It is important to emphasize that this was done not to fall into the error, all too frequent today, of thinking that the social state--with which it has been actively made common cause, along with other tendencies and parties, and social democratic sectors--would have become the model which depleted or shaped the proposals of all the socialists of that time. The truth is that, from this perspective, the always clear and ongoing accusation leveled against it was that it had great inherent inconsistencies and limitations and that it involved for the Third World, as was soon to rise to the surface, a high degree of dependency and submission. In addition, the detractors of the social state pointed out the international scale of the Cold War from which it took its cues, and concurrently the grave risk of alienating consumers and technocrats at whose cost the relative integration of certain sectors of the working class in the system was a built-in or given factor. But perhaps, in the last analysis, the social state, the "Welfare State" was the best organization that then as well as now, could be a formative part of the capitalism nowadays in force which, in its own right, came to be rebaptized as neocapitalism. By no means can one say that this was the organizational model, nor the state resulting from socialist guidelines, although it was thought that through authentication and profound study (i.e. by making it more truly democratic) it could progressively be able to achieve quantitative and qualitative steps in this always free and open historical process into which, as far as the democratic socialists were concerned, the much debated Marxian phase of the conversion of the state, and of the society in transition was being genuinely instrumented.[4]

The crisis of the managerial interventionist state, which was to a certain degree redistributive, the Welfare State, the state of service and social rights, has thus been the crisis of that "old paradigm." Accordingly, the attempt to mobilize public institutions to do something--despite capitalism--to foster a greater equality, a certain relative equality, an organization of social security and of protection of certain economic, labor, and cultural rights, which, until the intervention of the social state had been abandoned to the "free" interplay of the market forces and to the availability of each one of them. The growing increase in the demands of basic needs by greater outreaching social sectors, a claim accepted from the beginning for it implied an expanding nucleus of integration and legitimacy has, as a matter of course, led to the great fiscal crisis of this state model once there occurred a break in the facility of accumulation coming especially from the exploitation of the Third World. The growth and fulfillment of the social state has shown itself to be clearly contradictory in its private mode of production and appropriation. The crisis has been made worse (something which is hardly mentioned) by the enormous and insane increase in public funds brought about by the absurd arms race in which nations affiliated with political blocs have been engaged throughout the past years.

The state which makes social demands in times of abundance and growth in order to foster, in a dualistic contradictory manner, on the one hand both citizens who are freer and possess even more equal status among themselves and on the other manipulated consumers who are always insatiable, has found its capabilities depleted in those sectors. The unstoppable escalating military costs and increasing public attention to private accumulation of resources have also contributed to this depletion. The "old paradigm" based on the belief of unlimited economic growth and on the priority that certain sectors and classes placed on the efficiency of spending and squandering of money, on competition, on personal, social, national and international security, came to be increasingly replaced in the minds and aspirations of a more enlightened "left," in a more peremptory manner in the wake of the years following the beginning of the crisis, as Claus Offe underlines. From the end of the sixties there appeared a "new paradigm" which emphasized the values of growth (more qualitative than quantitative). Its focus was more on the quality of life, the protection of the environment, the satisfying of all basic needs, freedom, culture, ecology, etc.

The "actors," the subjects of the old paradigm, were almost uniquely the juridico-political institutions: the government, parliament, political parties as well as economic corporations and unions more or less integrated into the system. The "actors" of the "new paradigm" were fundamentally the new social movements. From the political point of view, the old paradigm of institutions is embodied in its more progressive manifestations, in the framework of social democracy. The new paradigm is characterized by a strong libertarian orientation.

What actually happened is that that new paradigm, which came into being for certain solid reasons among important sectors of the left, had in no way come to give rise to a tangible substitution of the old paradigm of the social state. On the contrary, what has really happened is that this paradigm has largely been substituted by, or at least has succumbed before the old paradigm which is part and parcel of the very conservative, neo-liberal state that at all costs aspires to prevail today, even in spite of the attempt made to reactualize the new paradigm. As far as this paradigm is concerned, only its anti-institutional mistrust has lent itself to its utilization and distortion in the hands of the neo-conservative ideology. This attitude has set in motion a policy of the state's non-intervention in economic matters. The less progressive elements are also involved in this, that is to say those who represent puritanical morality and those residues of pockets of benighted and rural-minded romantics who represent an uncritical and anti-philosophical bent of mind found among the upholders of reactionary and traditional views on values pertaining to education, family and sexuality. It is this amalgam of a technocratic establishment shunning critical and philosophical tenets, clinging to an absolute lack of ethics in the political and economic fields for the purpose of instituting unbridled capitalism and uncaring individualism, the cause out of which there arises the ever present and ever prevailing warmongering mindset.

This is what is now actually taking place, and before this display of the all-embracing and absolute power of the military-industrial complex, disguised ideologically as a liberal "minimal state," the attempts to maintain with some dignity the old social state, let alone to understand somehow the reality of libertarian utopias, are held down. It is necessary to examine with an independence of critical perspective the "new paradigm to avoid its claim of absolutization and of illegitimate correlative and ineffective negation of some of the valid elements which, when transformed, could very well be recouped to reinvigorate the "old paradigm." I am referring to the principal juridico-political institutions of pluralist and democratic society, which must be constantly authenticated and studied with the attentive gaze of the critic's eye in relation to civil society.[5]

Precisely because of those essential insufficiencies of some theoretical and practical manifestations of the new and old paradigms, is why I have been proposing the need and complementary usefulness of a "third paradigm," that of democratic socialism, which would bring together the reductional factors of both the old social-democratic paradigm and the new one that is libertarian by nature, i.e. one which is formed by taking into account the critical interrelationship of democratic-political institutions and the functional basic movements of civil society. This method seems to be the one that most harmoniously and aptly combines socialism with democracy. Virgilio Zapatero has insistently stated that there is a present-day need to take viable efficient action through the social state by means of a stronger presence and effectiveness of intermediary associations which comprise the whole fabric of the social edifice.

The state could do much of what it does a lot better and society today is wont to take different stands. One of the problems is that within "society" there are very disparate and even contradictory things: from powerful corporations to new social movements which include a growing number of more or less spontaneous self-governing organizations of every kind. The great social pact requires, as we shall later see, making crystal-clear who makes allocations, and how they are made, to the competing groups, that is, what is the state's function in the organization or coordination of all those social forces and sectors, and what is the best distribution for carrying out the interest or general well-being of the people. On this hinges the differences between the conservative ideology (more freedom for corporations, and as a logical consequence more freedom for the largest ones) and the socialist ideology (according to which both some or all of us, through the intermediacy of the democratic state or through that of a self-governing collective organization, take part in freely planning the freedom of every single one of us). Of course the difference in method also implies decisive differences in the objectives that can be coherently proposed and, more so, in those which can be realistically achieved.

But there are several things regarding the social state and I am considering them now in light of what Virgilio Zapatero insistently proposes. Firstly, the current state is too small for big things (which requires that it transfer part of its sovereignty and capacity to act to public organizations of international scope) and too big for small things (thus justifying its need to return part of its sovereignty to autonomous entities or communities whose character is national, regional or local). Secondly, the state does not have any reason to take direct charge of the production of all kinds of goods and services, including those which, because of their nature (but not only due to the benefits they offer), can be better handled by private enterprises or self-governing social organizations either exclusively or in shared efforts, which can also function in a non-controlled market. Thirdly, the state must take charge of and not abandon under any circumstance the key sectors of production which are considered most appropriate (and not only because they may be losing money) for that kind of organization and production. Fourthly, the decisive action that it ought to take will be through the medium of democratic planning for determining how funds should be allocated to competing groups. This I believe has something to do with socialism and, of course, with what is established in our Constitution.

The preferable goal, the inescapable requirement of a well-run social state in our time, is the attainment through different channels, on the part of the individual, of certain basic needs, that provide real satisfaction in the procurement of which comes to bear an understandable and rationally expansive criterion. This could be the most concrete application today of the rule of equality laid down for a state and for a democratic society, in addition to the indispensable equality before the law. But, in turn, it seems completely just, under current conditions, that this state keep the strict gratuitousness of certain goods and services as well as its strict preferential attention to less favored social sectors, to the most disadvantaged and worse off people, as a way of making progress through positive deeds toward satisfying those legitimate needs, and upgrading levels in order to serve the cause of greater equality. That the state, besides achieving a basic equality for all (equality for citizens who continue being the victims of inequality), the state would try to establish, in keeping with widespread norms, a condition of inequality for unequal citizens but one which would be the inverse of traditional inequality in that it would make provisions for setting up the unequals as equals. In my opinion, the exercise of freedom and the right to be different are also values which, within limits, must be preserved and maintained in any event.

The problem is how to organize in each concrete situation the great political and economic-social pact. Such a pact will obviously not fail to take into consideration, on the one hand, the empirical existence of certain de facto powers and superior forces of the means of production that are in place and, on the other hand, the democratic requirements or the popular will freely expressed through the decision of voters who gain a majority of votes at the polls. From the complex interrelationship of each concrete circumstance of these and other elements, which operate in the spheres of civil society or political institutions, will arise different possibilities, different modalities and typologies of that great political and economic social pact.

Perhaps all of this could be represented in the following diagram in which are also indicated, at the risk of being too schematic, the main inflections, "actors," subjects or institutions and organizations which predominate in each one of those concrete possibilities, always within, and this must be made clearly understood, that great common framework. The different pacts are only different modalities--but in no way do they lack importance and meaning, within that great general, social and constitutional pact.

The New Social Pact

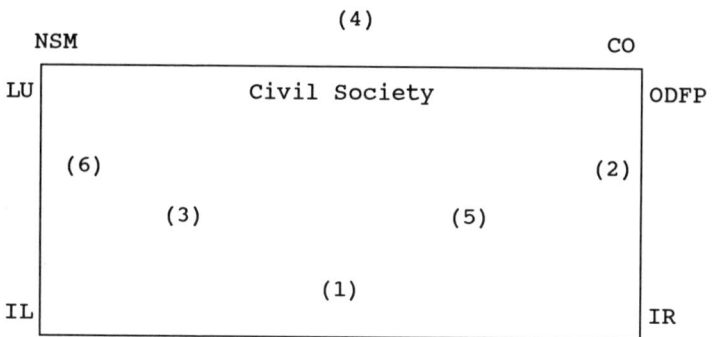

Components or principal "actors" (besides the ones indicated by abbreviations, among which would be located different political institutions on one side and on the other, and a greater or lesser plurality of "intermediate associations"):

IR	=	Institutional Right	IL	=	Institutional Left
CO	=	Corporations	LU	=	Labor Unions
ODFP	=	Old De Facto Powers	NSM	=	New Social Movements

Taxonomy of the pact:

Pact (1)	Basic institutional-constitutional pact
Pact (2)	IR and CO + OCDFP
Pact (3)	IL and CO + OCDFP
Pact (4)	Non-institutional social pact
Pact (5)	IR and LU + NSM
Pact (6)	IL and LU + NSM

Although there is not much mystery about what is outlined above, one can even figure out the subjects and the orientations of the pacts, which at the present time strike harmony with the democratic socialism that I espouse here and it would be well to repeat that in so doing consideration is given to the current constitutionality in which these facts are framed. Perhaps it is not amiss to impart some brief explanatory warnings and other assessments and critiques so as to have an overview of the matter at hand.

The first and principal point to emphasize is that this scheme does not contain two "legitimacies," one institutional and the other social, with the evident risk of grave dysfunctions and even of the loss of legitimacy. I would say that the fundamental legitimacy is one of the social origin, and is expressed in the institutional pact (1), which in turn is the basis of the constitutional pact, taking into account all it implies and all that it contributes to in its relationship with civil society. To some degree that pact (1) could therefore be called an institutional-constitutional pact, or perhaps it would be more to the point to call it preconstitutional and constituent. But in affirming that pluralist and representative institutional democracy, its insufficiency also seems certain to me if it is isolated and split off from civil society or from some of its most dynamic and progressive sectors. There is need then for a democracy of economic-social character and scope. This democracy by all means must find embodiment in the framework of the Constitution. Therefore, I insist on the importance of viewing the Constitution as a zone of convergence, as a factor of mediation, between a democratic theory of legitimacy and a critical theory of justice.[6]

Other questions which one might delve into at length here are those dealing with the complex meaning of the term "civil society," which today is once more so frequently used and even abused.[7] But I cannot go into a deep examination of all that which is behind that concept, that is to say from the different standpoints of Hobbes, Locke and Rousseau (as well as from the standpoints of those who preceded and followed these thinkers) inasmuch as the center of focus is, for better or for worse, the "condition of nature," as a condition of "society" (political or not), thereafter passing through the stages of the Hegelian "association of citizens" and the Marxian inversion of social classes.[8]

I use the term "civil society"--perhaps it would have been more prudent to leave it just as "society" or as something more precise like "fabric of society" or simply as economic and social organizations which are not strictly political--to signify the place or the quarters of organizations so diverse as those "old de facto powers," the economic and professional corporations, the labor unions and the "new social movements." Amid them is found that framework of self-governing organizations or associations that are neither governmental nor institutional and have very different goals in such areas as culture, charity, education, and sports. These organizations are a necessary complement today of the social state, and in some measure they have always played an active role in the concrete conditions of historical societies, much greater in some societies than in others. For example, their role is much greater in England than in Spain.

In that context of complex interrelationships between political institutions and civil society (or organizations that are primarily economic and social) is where those possible diverse types of pacts take place which, in the final result, fashion and shape the character, the meaning and the orientation of what we can now unproblematically denominate as a whole, that is to say, the "concrete social totality."

The basis is the institutional and constitutional pact (1) in which is concretized the fundamental conduct of constituent power. From that moment on, we witness the initiation of the action and the politics of the constituted powers driven by popular sovereignty and the rule of the majorities. According to the nature of these majorities, the direction of the pact will be able to and will have to correspond to the institutional right or left or to the center, or to coalitions formed by all or some of them. All of which is gradual, although symbolized here only in the few that are designated as institutional right and left. Pact (2) expresses the "natural" government (the natural majority) of the right, with greater or lesser leaning toward consensus also involving intermediate associations and even seeking some kind of understanding with unions that is not at all easy to achieve. There may be some kind of complementary relationship between pacts (2) and (5) insofar as in the latter the right also seeks support for its program in the anti-modern and anti-industrial "romantic-rural" sector, which occurs, for example, when there is confusion in the associations, and as a result it has found some place amid the broad spectrum of the so-called "new social movements." [9]

A risk inherent in the institutional pact (1) is its tendency toward the negative temptation of excluding everything from itself, or, in its most progressive aspect, of excluding all that is noninstitutional, that is to say, the great coalition which could be achieved in a de facto manner among parties of huge majorities but of varying significance within the spectrum of the "parliamentary establishment." This is being done frequently and I think that this constitutes a great error, at the cost of excluding from pact (1) the ample sectors of civil society, precisely those groups which have more advanced demands and the most marginal ones among those that form the so-called "new social movements." A similar exclusion and one with more harmful implications is accomplished in pact (3) when it is the institutional left which, for different reasons or because of some circumstances, concludes a pact with the most conservative sectors of the social body-politic (great economic corporations and old established institutions, giving low priority to union demands as well as the sometimes dissimilar demands of marginal sectors). [10]

A counterpoint, which is also reductionist, of the institutional pact (1) when the political power is separated from civil society and eliminates movements at their foundations, is brought about when both civil society and these movements, as happens in most social organizations, accept and make a part of themselves the above-mentioned situation but invert it by confirming--this is the case of pact (4)--the preference for or the absolute need of attaining several objectives of different characteristics. These objectives come to a head via exclusive social action and the elimination (or pretense of elimination) of the juridical-political institutions of the state. The spectrum of pact (4), one which we could call "liberal-libertarian," is enormously ambiguous and creates dangerous confusion, but the real fact is that both sectors coincide too frequently in the ideology which postulates the rejection of almost all criticism directed at the institutions of the current social state. It is nothing more than the same old story of the inevitable and insurmountable evil of the state, and, conversely, of the possibility of establishing a sound and effective state through an idyllic civil society. The liberals, or perhaps it would be better to say the neoliberal conservatives who are exclusively economists, know the objectives very well--those of capitalism--in seeking the minimal state and the diminution of state intervention (except for the protection of property and the security of the market). Its model of society is not the defense of freedom but that of capital. The libertarians are quite different from the neoconservatives; the former represent the old and pacifist libertarian view of anarchism, although there also existed a violent type of libertarian who supported the idea of "direct action" from the leftist perspective. I refer to those libertarians characterized by pacific social and union action when I assert that their work is a full realization of the concept of freedom, which is inseparable from equality. I think, nevertheless, that their ways of acting exclusively on social and cultural matters ought, in their attempt to achieve those very objectives, be in tune with a practical application through a path which is also institutional, a combination that I have been proposing in these pages as the most appropriate and specific way of attaining democratic socialism.

The path that I support is pact (6) preferably entered into between the institutional left and broad sectors of civil society, grass-root associations which promote and instrument their own policies with differing aims, and in a very special way, unions and progressive and marginal sectors that form part of the new social movements. It is wholly certain that these sectors do not present de facto demands that are always harmonious; on the contrary, they are frequently at logger-heads and contradict one another. It is also certain that what is social is not always rational--the same holds true for the institutional--and, therefore, criticism and self-criticism are, in both spheres and at every moment, completely necessary. The rationality of democratic legitimacy and of the theory of justice must always take into account and evaluate both dimensions together, although democratic institutional legitimacy always provides the always indispensable basis for that ultimate rationality which is demanded of a critical theory of justice.

Thus, given that the institutional-constitutional pact (1) had electoral support accrued to it, from a pact (6) broadened to increase all the sectors of civil society, participants in such a project will have recourse to frame democratic socialism by unifying the rest of the pacts into a single one. Among them, of course, the one that also incorporates and integrates into the totality all the "corporations" (mixed economic ones) and the organisms and entitles which I have designated until now, in a pejorative way, as being "old de facto powers," which in turn would gain a fair share of legitimacy and even ethical justification.

I definitely think that in these coordinates and in similar ones related to them is where one can find, as I said at the beginning, a social and cultural basis sufficient to overcome in a progressive sense, that is to say in favor of liberty, equality and solidarity in the current crisis of legitimacy of the welfare state, a crisis which can affect the whole social state, including the democratic state itself. That new social contract can and must be the basis for a legality which gives it expression on solid grounds of a well-founded legitimacy, that of a justice which is historical and concrete, and always capable of being made more perfect, reinforced in the long run, with broader and more efficient support for social legitimacy.

NOTES

[1] Claus Offe, *New Social Movements: Challenging the Boundaries of Institutional Politics* (Department of Sociology, University of Bielefeld, 1985), p. 14 and ff. and republished in *Social Research* (publication of the New School for Social Research in New York) 52.4 (1985) 817-69. My study uses Offe's ideas as a base and stimulus for the development of my own thoughts on the subject.

[2] Although the welfare state and the social state have an intimate relationship, they are not coincidental. On this matter and also on the origins and meaning of both and related questions, see the recent Spanish books: Carlos de Cabo Martín, *La crisis del Estado Social* (Barcelona: Promocionces Publicaciones Universitarias, 1988), Ramón García Cotarelo, *Del Estado del bienestar al Estado del malestar* (Madrid: Centro de Estudios Constitucionales, 1986) and Josep Pico, *Teorías sobre el Estado del Bienestar* (Madrid: Siglo XXI, 1987). Two recent books in English are: Charles I. Schottland, ed., *The Welfare State: Selected Essays* (New York: Harper Torchbooks, 1967) and Ramesh Mishra, *The Welfare State in Crisis* (Brighton: Wheatsheaf Books, 1984).

[3] See especially my book *Estado del derecho y sociedad democrática* (Cuadernos para el Diálogo, 1966) which incorporated several previous studies of mine. I continue to support the proposal in that book for a socialist democratic state of law.

[4] For a clarification of my position on this matter, see the third chapter ("Marx y la teoría marxiana del Derecho y del Estado" in my book *De la maldad estatal y la soberanía popular*, (Madrid: Debate, 1984).

[5] Virgilio Zapatero, *El futuro del Estado social* in the series *El futuro de socialismo* (Madrid: Editorial Síntesis, 1966) p. 65 and ff.

[6] See my book, *Legitimidad y justicia: La Constitución, zona de convergencia*, (Alicante: University of Alicante, "Doxa," no. 4, 1987).

[7] To get a good idea of these questions, one should read Salvador Giner's important book *Ensayos civiles* (Barcelona: Ediciones Península, 1987), especially chapter 2, which deals with the changes of civil society, and chapter 3 regarding class, power and privilege in corporative society. The other chapters have also been useful in the development of this article.

[8] In the recent Spanish bibliography on some of these questions, studied through comparative analysis that used the models of Montesquieu and Rousseau, we point out the useful, well-documented and well-structured essay of María del Carmen Iglesias, *Los cuerpos intermedios y la libertad en la sociedad civil* (Alcalá de Henares: Instituto de Administración Pública, 1986).

[9] Claus Offe, in his *New Social Movements* (cited in note 1) pp. 43, 70 and 80 among others, situates within the framework of the so-called "new social movements" three well differentiated sectors. The first one consists of a new middle class composed of intellectuals, technicians and professionals trained preferably at universities, who are the main social substratum of ecologists, pacifists, feminists and other groups. The second comprises "non-mercantile" marginal sectors, that is those who are situated outside of the market place, for example, the unemployed, housewives, retired people, those living on pensions, ethnic groups that suffer from discrimination and so forth. Finally, there are the remnants of old middle class people who have an agrarian mentality, that is those who are romantic-rural, anti-

industrial, and fear technical advances. This third sector is the one which, in the scheme I am developing here, would link that pact (5) with the institutional right. Unlike his previous works, Offe's *New Social Movements* now sees being more possible the alliance between those first two sectors of new social movements and the institutional left. This would be pact (6), in my opinion. Although I have used Offe's latest work as a point of departure for my own analysis, as I stated in footnote 1, my proposal would be more along the lines of a total foundation of the global political and social pact in terms of legitimacy and justice. Therefore, together with the new social movements, I would also consider other segments and intermediate associations of the so-called civil society which Offe, taking a more radical position, does not, to my mind, take into account the pact with the institutional left.

[10]See my monograph No. 80-81 published by the journal *Sistema* (Madrid, November, 1987), which bears the title *Estado de bienes y opciones de política económica*.

[Translation of an article published in *Estudios de Deusto* (Bilbao), 37 (July-December, 1989)]

JOSE JIMENEZ LOZANO

José Jiménez Lozano was born in Avila in 1930. He has university degrees in law, letters and journalism. This writer has published many articles in newspapers and magazines throughout Spain and is the author of a dozen collections of essays and eight novels and narratives. In his works he shows his interest in the Spanish Inquisition, Jews, Moors, converts to Catholicism, Spanish art and the architecture, and the Bible. He published *Los grandes relatos (The Great Narrations)* in 1991. In 1988 he won the Literary Prize of Castile and León for his complete work and in 1989 he won the National Prize of Criticism.

THE DANGER OF REMINISCING AND THE ENSUING TALES

It may be said that what best defines the most significant aspect of our culture right now and the way in which man appears installed in it, is that for the first time we are not nor do we wish to be "a conscience implied in stories."[1] The tale or narration of what has occurred and of reminiscence which was from the beginning the privileged instrument of the knowledge of the world and of the human condition--"the rhapsodic beginning" of thought about which Kant wrote--has been displaced from both scientific history and the literary fable by technical and formal expedients, directed toward objectivism.

Neither history nor literary narration must have a plot any longer, and the art of telling has stopped being the essential aspect of writing history or narrating, rather, it has become greatly suspected as being one of the worst acts of wrongdoing. The modern narrator is solemnly entreated and summoned to the search of a new language and new images to celebrate "the new pleasures of living" in an urban and secular society. And Michel Ignatieff, who believes that language will have to find itself and raise itself from the laments over the alienation of modern life, encountered in the images of Hopper's New York, Joyce's Dublin, Musil's Vienna, Bellow's Chicago and Kundera's Prague, without "some escape to another place and another time,"[2] strangely brings to mind Voltaire's observations on Pascal's *Thoughts*. "For me, Voltaire writes, when I look at Paris or London, I see no reason to enter that state of despair that Pascal speaks of. I see a city that does not seem a desert by any stretch of the imagination, but one that is populated, opulent, and clean, in which men are happy as much as their human nature permits. What wise man would fill himself with despair because he does not know the nature of his thought and only knows some attributes of matter?"[3]

But this is not what could torment us at all now, and everybody seems especially content for having exorcised the memory of the past, together with those metaphysical preoccupations, and the living from hand to mouth, looking forward to a magnificent future. History and the past, contemplated in such a way, as something definitively split from and outside our knowledge of Modernity, cause fear and produce a militant rejection in us. Our own time has seen, with its carnal eyes, the industrial abattoir, the image of which the ideologies and the theories of metaphysics have assumed, and which, in one way or another, have ontologized the past or converted history into the supreme judge of truth and of human destiny, so that it has lost its taste for the very name of history, or is frightened on hearing it, and rejects it as being loathsome. As Herman Melville, we have had to face whales "with these visible hands," and those whales were the Leviathan of history and its armies, its messianic visions of redemption or of a kingdom of one thousand years for a race of supermen. While its epic narrations made contact and were interwoven with the other old dazzling "Great Tales" which in the course of time also had fascinated men, driving them mad with dreams and hopes, and to an equal extent subdued them with "the sound and fury," with horror and death. Consequently, one does not want to know anything about those "Great Tales," and stories clothed in purple which inevitably carry hidden in their folds a great design: the claim of an absolute truth. Therefore, we take refuge in the short "fragmentary tales without greater aspirations--above all without any claim of truth--as contained in only private documents."[4] Our own thinking must become "frail": that is, suspicious and mistrustful of claiming some type of truth out of fear that it don the scarlet uniform of the church officials of past centuries, and indeed we would be visited in the early hours of the morning in our own dwelling place, by agents of the political police or constables of some inquisition, which, as Ionesco says, with good reason, is what has happened only too frequently in history.

But what if there never had been "Great Tales," what if truth had never donned the purple or scarlet and never had the assistance of constables to bring home its point?

Truth as Derision

In reality, there have never been "Great Tales" and the truth has only made its historic appearance as misfortune and ridicule, as a pitiful vagrant who is standing before the magistrate and does not understand what is being said to him, nor know what to say. And, "if through his stammering," writes Simone Weil, "there pours out of his mouth some soul-rendering utterings, they will not be heard by the magistrate or those who are present. It is a silent shout."[5] It cannot be understood: "justice is no longer a matter of the gods but something which cannot be told and its horizon is the world."[6] But, because of that, truth can only be manifested thus: in absurdity and paradox, "in the fact that it is hidden," said Kierkegaard.[7] And the humble condition of God's manifestation in the crucified Christ ("See what kind of man he is!" added Kierkegaard) has always been the expression of "truth" in the theology of the cross and that of the concealed God. Later it was institutionalized Christianity which has been inclined to favor a theology of glory or has seen itself compelled to do so as it has chosen to gain historical relevance and has cloaked "truth" in purple and power converting it into a political and ecclesiastic "Great Tale." And Christianity seems today like an ecclesiastic "Great Tale" of the past: "the survival of the past, unmodified in the present, its prolongation beyond its own time," says Leszek Kolakowski.[8] But Christianity, as the "madness of the cross" or buffoonery is a "murmur" and "a silent shout" opposed to that Great Tale. "In the topsy-turvy attitude of the buffoon," L. Kolakowski continues, "his voice says what is only a possibility and what seems real to him, before it comes into existence. Our thoughts about reality are also a part of that reality and not worse than the other parts."[9]

The "theology of the buffoon" is a "theology of the cross" and theology is the conception of truth as a vagrant standing before the judge: a Kierkegaardian theology of paradox and shock. But it seems to me that it is in this sphere of things that theology ultimately airs the issue of mistrust and rejection of the "Great Tale," as well as of history. Modernity seeks to crush the infamous behavior which characterizes Christianity. It is the insufferable central "Great Tale."

It is important to emphasize right now, in keeping with the Kierkegaardian view of the matter, the "auditive" and narrative nature of truth which is discerned in an absurd and paradoxical manifestation, rendering it opaque. Kierkegaard assimilates "the scandal" of the paradox perceived as a resonance, to the "acoustic illusion" which does not understand the exact sonority of the narration (the Word). The only possibility of capturing it is to have each listener put himself in what is called "the situation," the integration in the "contemporaneity" of what is related.

And these categories are theological, but, as has been said, they offer the most profound and most serious dimension of what constitutes a tale: an expressive form, a way of knowledge, "a literary genre" that has its origin in the sphere of biblical culture and with this one must, in whichever attempt one undertakes to arrive at a solution, and take into account such particulars as memory, remembrance, and history.[10]

And There Were Never "Great Tales"

But what is certain is that there were never "Great Tales." From the very beginning the brief and daily testimonies of private existence were the first and only instruments of access for knowing about the world and mankind. The "Great Tales" which not only at this moment in time but throughout the ages have always frightened men and caused them to rise against them and even destroy them, have never really been tales or narrations but intellectual, ideological, political, moral or sacral systems or ideograms. In short, these "Great Tales" were more often than not based on old true and humble stories whose "very frail" truth they revised, deformed or used for their own purposes and whose formal structure they usurped or parodied. Albeit they are only ersatz stories like the fairy tales which, begin with the words: "once upon a time," and cannot be pinned down in any definable place or time. Myths, for example, are not stories in their deceiving formal appearance for there is nothing historical in them. What is narrated in them has not happened in history; one could say that they consist of what has happened to gods, and thus, outside of worldly history, time and space. The only element of narration in them is the suffering that they have caused men, and which men have set down for the sake of remembrance.

There have never been "Great Tales" because men have always commented on their condition when observing the strangeness and wonder of the world or the hostility of nature, or have narrated to us the happiness and suffering of life, and the injustice and the pain that has afflicted them, or their hopes of freeing themselves from pain and suffering always have been expressed through short and fragmentary stories of everyday life. They have been atrocious testimonies as well as simple comical statements which memory recounts. For example, in the Spain of Philip II, the epic "Great Tale" of the empire in whose dominions the sun never set existed alongside the terse stories that the common people inherited from their ancestors as well as accounts taken from their own experience of suffering and hunger.

A people even employed, as has been said, the fragmentary, ordinary and everyday narration to speak of their invisible God, whose name is unpronounceable and "totally different" or, rather, it felt itself obliged to do so, inventing the "literary genre" of telling stories, because their God was involved in the daily circumstances of their nomadic life, in the abundance and scarcity of grass for grazing, in weddings and childbirth, in love and friendship, tragic juvenile deaths and the placid deaths of old people who had lived a full life, in all planes of human existence. Their scribes and narrators have told us this and the Book in which these stories are found is essentially the totality of these stories together with threads of history and some extraordinary poems.

In rereading and retelling these stories, at least in their cultural sphere or religious tradition, as happens in the Story of "Pesach" or Passage through the Red Sea, which is a story of suffering and liberation, those who recount it are led by virtue of the narration itself to put themselves into "that time and place" and to hope that what happened then would happen again. Every memory and every story are defined here in their essence and "newness," while the essence of the "Great Tale," which does not relate anything, is the exact repetition, the "survival of the unmodified past in the present, its prolongation beyond itself" and produces the boredom and terror, a monotonous but prestigious and powerful manifestation which seeks the submission of those who are exposed to it.

History without Scarlet

But if there never have been "Great Tales," but always only short and fragmentary tales in which we now seek refuge. While we are not even bold enough to suggest that they offer some claim to be true, because truth wrapped in purple or scarlet frightens us, this was not the case when they first made their appearance. It may turn out that the torment of history, the past of horror and constriction, is not exactly the scarlet woman of the Apocalypse or her secular likeness which is equally deceiving and bloody. Perhaps, in any case, there are several histories or another history which has not spoken or has spoken like the vagrant standing before the judge: stammering and with a "silent shout." Thus, the entire past will not be capable of being removed at one glance, excised from our awareness of Modernity, renounced and liquidated as quick as possible, or "guillotined." In reality, after a very summary judgment in which Modernity sat on the tribunal ontologizing itself and also being very absolute about the future, created from that time onward in its own image, planned in a supreme gesture of abolition of history which was to be but not become, because its great options would be determined from the "now," a powerful new "truth," a "strong thought," a new "Great Tale," exactly equal to the old ones: that of Progress and Reason.

The other history--with a lower case "h"--is nevertheless there: since it does not carry the mantle of scarlet, it does not shine. In reality, it never wore any mantle: perhaps only a coat of rags, if it had anything at all to cover itself with, and like all the hapless beings it turned out to be invisible, as Hölderlin has shown us. But that history is there, as if it were the incurable sore which the Great History has on its side under the purple garb, like the "gnawing worm" of Reason, the filthy suburb of Voltaire's marvelous city. And what can one do with it? What can it mean if one wants to say something or be right?

Walter Benjamin does not care at all about this inconvenience regarding History, with a capital "H," and neither does it concern him in the case of Reason, Enlightenment, Progress and Modernity. He evokes that "history of world suffering" which "is the means of the fulfillment of reason and freedom," and which Metz says is in clear critical opposition to the trivial idea which is unthinkable, that of "a non-dialectic progress of reason."[11] And Benjamin's *Angelus Novus (New Angel)* "does not lose the face of the past," although "it is true that the face of the angel, according to Reyes Mate, seems utterly terrified by what he sees, which seems to mean that the one who speaks today so lightly of happiness does so because he does not dare to look backward," and because he forgets--or does he want to forget?--that "only through love of those without hope have we been given hope," Benjamin recalls. This is to say, he forgets that "only if the present generations seek for themselves the liberation of past generations can they reverse the present and hope for something different from what they already have."[12]

And so it is. But, if it is so, that says very clearly which is the remembrance that matters: "dangerous" reminiscing and the ensuing tales. They are dangerous because their "silent shouts" can begin to speak and to say something new and terrible, or dazzling and full of hope.

In the very act of reminiscing, in the pure operation of invoking the past as was always done, in the "Great Tales" and the "Great History" or in its literary summarizations, the presumptions or similes of stories written against the background reference of "blackened water," and which always and only point toward the same thing,"[13] are carried forth precisely to invoke the past, the solid and powerful past which is at hand as a "dogmatic certainty" because it has left a document or testimony and vestiges of its power. And furthermore, in the nostalgic dream of that past and in its pleasant and morbid or glowing narration, what is sought is to cause to resound even more strongly, the permanence of the "Great Tale," the parcel of authority which social transformations have carried forth, or in their sovereign and unique passage through time, which is eternally repeatable and must be repeated, do not resound enough. I believe that in Proust as well as in Thomas Mann or in Balzac, always where there is literary greatness and splendor, there will be present that more or less conscious drive toward ontological meaning, toward wordly power and value, which the writer espouses.

Everything will have to continue being that way, and Simone de Beauvoir has shown us how Balzac could not consider a woman as a female human being if she did not fit the mold of a damsel or a woman of the bourgeoisie. It was impossible for him to recognize that those "beings" belonged to the human species, exactly as Borges confessed that same impossibility in reference to the proletariat or sub-proletariat. And that is a perfectly understandable and unavoidable result since those narrators as so many others, especially historians, have until very recent times taken the point of view of the masters and conquerors of history, those who have conformed and have left a trace in it. Those legions of people who had not had a protagonistic role in history had scarcely begun to be heard of in the writing or annals of history. And this being the case, "in the act of reminiscing only the predominant state of affairs is confirmed, which is that of the conqueror." But "by this system of appropriation of the past there is no way of understanding history in all its anachronistic, painful or unsuccessful aspects,"[14] as W. Benjamin says. There will only be one road for this understanding: "any utopia or idea of a better future goes through a change in the present and that is only possible through the recovery of the unique past which is no longer there since it has failed or "it has to feed itself with the image of the humble ancestors."

The obsession of historicism that consists of the idea that nothing should be lost and that the whole past be preserved is frustrated by the assumption that the whole past is lost. It does no good to resort to modernizing tales, which historicism tries to do in order to recover the past. Only if one passes from one conception of history as a science to the other one of history as reminiscing can the past be saved from oblivion. Indeed, "what science posits as confirmed can be altered by reminiscence. It can make us consider what we thought as finished, as unfinished, and open-ended, and what we considered to be unfinished turns out to be finished."[15]

And W. Benjamin adds: "This is theology," but through reminiscence we concoct an experience which prevents us from understanding history in a fundamentally atheological manner, although neither is it permitted us to attempt to explain it immediately with theological categories,"[16] which is exactly what happens to us with the tale. The narrated reminiscence and its potentiality to transform the present by making it contemporaneous with the past, through the contemporaneity attained by the one who remembers or by the listener or reader of the narrated reminiscence, cannot be understood atheologically, but neither is it permitted us to try to explain it as pure theology or as a pure theological category. The tale that is constitutively theological and is born in this ambience, as was said, is also essentially secular and not religious, but vis-à-vis each tale we have to question ourselves just as Th. Adorno posed the question regarding politics. He asserted that that what is not theological in politics is business, and by the same token that which is, is of necessity pure rhetoric, or comedy. Or still worse, a celebration of the "Great Tales," a memory of the dogmatic certainty of the past and an attempt at establishing the supremacy of the present. And Julien Benda has been able to say consequently that "artistic sensitivity is much more rewarded by a system which tends toward the realization of force and greatness, than by another which tends toward the establishment of justice." He adds that "artistic sensitivity is especially exalted by the spectacle of a mass of individuals, some of whom are subordinated to others, until one among them supremely rises to the forefront to dominate the rest."[17]

Midwives and Pharaohs, Young Ladies in Waiting and Kings

Thus the brief and ordinary narrations are there, not only for our own refuge, disillusioned as we are with the "Great Narrations," but as enlightenment and a gateway to knowledge. The reminiscence raises its frail truth like a dangerous subversion against the "Great History," and opens up to us the histories and memories of suffering or joy. They are minimal histories, reminiscences and narrations of daily occurrences that are so invisible and fragile. For example, the one that the narrator of the book of Exodus or of The Names, as it is called in Hebrew, tells us of Shiphrah and Puah [1:15], whose names mean "to be pretty" and to "be a girl."[18] They are not too individualized, which happens with all the "invisible" ones. But the narrator who tells us his story only has eyes for them amid the Egyptian splendors. He is blind to the splendors of pharaoh"s court and its buildings, clothing, jewels, or the elegant furniture and also to its fabulous burial ritual. He is not concerned about the names of the princes nor the glory of their deeds, the "Great Tales" kept for his scribes for "eternal memory." The only thing that counts for him is the short, minimal, clandestine story of those midwives who disobey pharaoh's order to kill each masculine child born to the Hebrews. When we hear such a story, it suddenly bursts into the universe of power and splendor of the pharaonic "Great Narration," and subverts and destroys it with the memory of that suffering and that hope of liberation from injustice. It brings us face to face with our own situation and makes us contemporaneous of that situation and of Shiphrah and Puah.

This view of the narrator about the Empire of the world which only notices those two women is, at the same time, an aesthetic option to recount its prettiest aspect, which in turn involves an ethical option which is the protest against injustice, its frustration and the dream of liberation. Or one can see it foremost as an ethical option which can only be expressed in a short narration and in it its beauty is revealed. In it judgment is passed on the magnificent tyranny of the pharaonic "Great Tale" and the truth it puts forth has the effect of tearing it to shreds because the modest tale is always truthful, a quality without which it cannot live. If this were not so, it would not be able to narrate a reminiscence of suffering or of hope, an ethical one which distinguishes between victim and cruel master, always disguised in the "Great Narration," without the truth provided by ethicality. And ethicality or "theology" is essential to the modest narration which recounts frustrations, sufferings or dreams, and cries out for them to have a final say, so that the formulation of suffering or of hope may lead to a happy ending, and justice and the pending account be settled now or in the future.

But Modernity, cut off from the past, does not expect a different future either, a time which is in the coming. It does not "follow the plotting" of what was or "could not be"; it is "the present moment," what is "instantaneous," a "fragment" of life, without memory or ethicality. If these things were one with what we term "the instantaneous," Modernity would become a narration and it would put its consistency at risk. This would happen because the memory of the past devastatingly bursts forth at the very instant of its penetration and in its condition of "established forever." "The memory of the past," writes H. Marcuse, can give rise to dangerous perspectives, and established society seems to distrust the subversive contents of memory. To remember is a way of separation of oneself from given events, a kind of intercession which, during brief instants, breaks the omnipresent power of what is factual. Memory brings to mind terror and past hopes . . . and the recollections of the individual and the anguish and yearnings of humanity creep into the personal events which are relived in the individual memory.[19]

"The candid snapshot," as it appears before our eyes, and as writers and artists have tried to capture it and fix it in their writings and paintings, becomes a tale and speaks. It narrates to us those plots on which silence has cast its spell. Thus does it begin to say what could not be said, what was not wanted to be said or what was not suspected that it would have been said by those who were thought to be wordless before such time as words were just in their mouths. And that is, for example, what occurs with *The Meninas* of Velázquez, a paradigm of what is "instantaneous" in art, of the sense of the instant in its awareness of modernity, according to Ortega.

Ortega said that Velázquez revolutionized painting by abandoning mythological and religious themes when he set out to paint everyday scenes. In the words of Ortega: "Art was a dream, a delirium, a fable, a convention, an ornament of formal grace. Velázquez asked himself whether it was possible to create art in this world and in life as it is. . . . [20] So it was that Velázquez began to paint daily life and the things related to it and his paintings "stopped being the generic representation of imaginary and otherworldly forms," and Ortega proceeds to note that in this manner Velázquez inaugurated modern painting. But this is not exactly so when one thinks of the identification of Christian religion with otherworldliness and mythology.[21] Ortega's non-theological culture did not permit him to suspect that perhaps Christianity was not exactly a religion, but that is what it is, an historically and not otherworldly religion, and, of course, not a mythology but a tale. Although the theological essence of the narrator also eluded

Ortega, which caused him to believe that Velázquez himself had secularized the evangelic scene painted in his work *Christ's Visit to the House of Mary and Martha* in order to narrate it.[22] In this picture Ortega saw the following: "a kitchen in which an old woman and a girl are busy preparing a meal. Neither Christ nor Martha nor Mary appear in the room, but there is a picture hung high on the wall and in this interior picture one sees the figures of Christ and the two holy women who constitute an unreal presence. In this way Velázquez declared himself not responsible for painting what cannot be painted, in his opinion. The ingeniousness of the solution shows us to what degree he had decided from his youth not to accept the artistic tradition that painting is the art of representing the implausible."[23]

The implausible? Have implausible things been represented only in painting Christian tales? And was Velázquez not placing himself in the time of Christ and Martha and Mary and thus making them our contemporaries when he painted the tale in this way?

In any case, Ortega's interest is in fleshing out Velázquez's modernity and secularism which are best illustrated in such paintings as *The Drunkards, Vulcan's Forge, The Lances,* and especially in *The Meninas*. Ortega wrote the following about this last mentioned painting: "[It] is any precise instant in the studio of a painter. Velázquez, by painting an instant in time, eternalized it, which is the mission of painting. In short, *The Meninas* is a painting in which a painter paints what is paintable."[24]

Yes, but the instant of painting passed and "the candid shot" is now the painting of a painter painting, or rather of a painter who assumes the pose of painting several human beings who narrate a plot. In reality, only through the plot, which mediates as though it were an invisible hard and solid plate, an engraving or illustration of the picture, can the viewer understand this. And what is certain is that the painting in question has given rise to such a great deal of surmisings that that glass plate has been enlarged in importance through explanations and interpretations to an extent that this picture, this "candid picture," can only be seen as deformed, which is perhaps what brings Jonathan Brown to say that *The Meninas* is a painting "as subtle as it is ambiguous," that if we try to explain the reason for its greatness, we will soon prove that it eludes any intuitive or rational understanding."[25] But surely a naive and inexperienced look at art, one that is interested in the intricacies of interpretation, can hardly be said to reap any benefit from viewing the "Great Candid Picture."

It is already established that that "Great Candid Picture" is presented to us as a "Great Tale" of the Spanish monarchical and Catholic baroque which shines for an instant in the painter's work. The artist is there, dressed for the occasion and wearing his Cross of Santiago. The monarchs enter the room and are seen reflected in the mirror, but at the same time they freeze the whole action which was taking place in the room. It is the aura of his Catholic Majesty which stops everything, and which, later, when photography made its appearance, would be called the "birdie": everything stops in attempting to see an invisible bird fly by. Two ladies of honor *(meninas)* in the court wait on the princess Margaret. One of them, the one who offers her water in a clay vessel, is María Agustina Sarmiento, and the other is Isabela de Velasco. And behind the latter is the *dueña, doña* Marcela de Ulloa, and near her, an unidentified figure who scholars tell us is the custodian of the palace bedrooms, and, in the background, opening the door toward a sun-filled gallery into which the monarchs will enter, is the chamberlain, don José Nieto. The room is inundated with light which enters through that door and in the foreground on the right there is a large dog and two unimportant figures who are not more important than the dog, though they do have an ornamental and functional value. They are María Bárbola and Nicolasillo Pertusato, two residents of the Royal Palace which lodged dwarfs, monsters, idiots and jesters called "vermin," which were strange creatures whose job was to entertain the princes and courtiers. These "vermin" are emitting a "silent shout," but with the whispering of their "memory of suffering" the candid picture is deconstructed and the real plot of what is represented there is introduced.

María Bárbola and Nicolasillo Pertusato "hapless beings" or "vermin," judge from the perspective of their wretchedness the "Great Tale" of the painting and of the time. They are Shiphrah and Puah in this other pharaonic court and universe, and in all the universes of the "Great Tales" of the world, including our own; they are the reminiscence of a great chain of ancestors humiliated like them, a chain of humiliation which must be broken now and not continued in the future. There they are looking at us, like the vagrant before the judge, trying to find the words that express the truth of their misfortune, which through external circumstances makes perceptible the shout always uttered in silence: Why do you harm me?[26]

But this woebegone lot know that they "ought not count on making their suffering known by men of talent, personalities, celebrities or even by the geniuses in the sense that the word genius is generally used, that is, when it is taken to mean talent. They can only count on geniuses of the highest order: the poet of the *Iliad*, Aeschylus, Sophocles, Shakespeare as he was when he wrote *Lear*, and Racine when he wrote *Phaedra*.[27] Only they, indeed, are capable of relating the reminiscences of misfortune and of silence, of invisible grief or hope, which are yet to arrive. We could add Cervantes, or Velázquez as he was, when without having to put up with being a member of the Order of Santiago because he did not expect to visit royalty and did not dream of fame, was kindly disposed toward dwarfs, jesters and idiots, the "bodies of whom were made to receive blows and carry out lowly tasks, bodies disseminated throughout time immemorial. They are there to perform as laughing-stocks."[28]

These suffering beings, belong to that tradition of downtrodden wretches that only narrators at the height of their genius can depict. Simone Weil says that because "misfortune is as horrible as the expression of misfortune is supremely beautiful,"[29] it is necessary that the story of that misfortune be absolutely beautiful. The tale must exorcise and avenge that misfortune and place the sufferer (that is, the one who dreams and laughs, and is excluded from the possession of property and power) in the center of the world, to capture history with a pen as the painter does with his brush in his *The Meninas*. As we already know, Velázquez accomplishes this, not by the entrance of the Monarchs but by the solemn presence of María Bárbola and Nicolasillo Pertusato and the whole chain of their "humbled ancestors."

Whether Velázquez realized it or not, the center of this picture is on the right as we face the painting. It is in the angle where the dog is lying, looking somewhat like a noble lion, near the "vermin."

Remembrance has altered the "Great Tale" of the painting. What seemed concluded in that "Great Candid Picture" remains open and is put into motion.

The Center of the World

This is always dealt with in the tale. "The respect which is owed to the accumulated suffering in history sensitizes reason," it makes reason so perceptive that it becomes unnecessary to express it in simple absolute contraposition involving "authority and knowledge," as is wont to be the hypothesis from which the debate over the autonomy of reason stems and from which there seems to stem the idea of emancipation as an "a priori" foundation of reason. Perceived in this way, history acquires, in its capacity as history evoked from suffering, the form of "dangerous tradition.... Its mediation is at any rate practical in nature and comes about through narrating 'dangerous stories' wherein the interest in freedom takes place, is identified and registered. This remembrance has an unavoidable narrative structure and the narrated or recounted reminiscence has a 'cognitive primacy'."[30]

We have already seen this. Not only does it subvert and destroy the "Great Tale" and "Great History" by laying them bare, but this makes us hear the silent remembrance or shout, the words not pronounced until then make what is narrated contemporary to us. It makes us escape from what is factual.

But the tale is dangerous above all, because it avenges the sufferer and compensates him for his suffering by making him the center of the world and placing on his shoulders the most beautiful purple cloth woven by men of genius as though it were woven in the very workshop of the woeful people he has represented. From viewing these people the revelation of the artist's identification with their suffering is thrust upon us. "An idiot of the people, in the literal sense of the word, who really loves truth, although he only makes stammering sounds, is in his thought infinitely superior to Aristotle. He is nearer to Plato than Aristotle ever was. He has genius, while for Aristotle only the word talent was suitable."[31]

And it has been frequently the case that village idiots have indeed been those who have narrated to us what was not among the well-known events of history, but buried in it. In their silence or laughter they have made audible to us all the possibilities which there, in their genius, are already real and must be so in the reality of existence. When these "vermin" tell us their stories they certainly find the most beautiful and appropriate form, since a narrator can only listen and learn, and then utilize the "barbarian language" which is not in conformance with the grammar of mystics, the harsh, elliptic language full of tropes and metasememes and "holes of silence," oxymoron and faulty pronunciation, or convoluted syntax. On the other hand, we encounter the greatest simplicity and conciseness: single words which are linked together internally. Monosyllables. Certeau says that the language of the mystics is an "artifact of silence," or is it an opaque but revealing language of knowledge? Perhaps both.

While the narration is heard or read, what is narrated in the story and about its protagonist center around the universe's navel. Shiphrah and Puah travel throughout the whole of Egypt, where the Empire and its glory are invisible, and in rereading their story now, the same thing happens with all the great things and events of the world. What happens specifically in the brief and fragmentary narrative is the paralysis of history, which the "Great Tales" have vainly tried to make eternal in a snapshot. While the "Great Tale" is repetitious, the narration is unique and unforgettable. It is always capable of becoming current and affecting us like an axe thrust to the head, or like a "disaster," as Kafka said to his friend Oskar Pollack, bringing to mind an allusion to tales in their capacity as such. It is, moreover, a miracle.[32]

Man's history has been a gushing of torment and of suffering or of hope, and the tale that avoided that ethical or theological condition of remembrance by virtue of evoking history as recreational, would not be much different from the recreational physics of the 18th-century salons, seeing that this was not a game but a pastime (in the Pascalian sense of escape) from dangerous reality. And in that sense, in that banality, it consisted of words sown in "blackened water," of a dead snapshot, a dead remembrance of the dead past, of the painting of *The Meninas* without María Bárbola and without Nicolasillo Pertusato. Another prestigious "Great Tale," a sacred whale once again, and as is the case, we have come against too many sacred and deadly whales with these visible hands.

NOTES

[1] Johan B. Metz, "Recuerdo," in *La fe en la historia y la sociedad* (Madrid: Cristiandad, 1979) 207.

[2] Michael Ignatieff, *The Needs of the Strangers* (New York: Penguin Books, 1988) 141.

[3] "Voltaire," "Remarques," in Saint-Beuve, "*Port Royal* vol. 2 (Paris: "La Pléiade" Gallimard, 1954) 362.

[4] Manuel Reyes Mate. "Jiménez Lozano y Umberto Eco, dos historias del pasado," *El País*, 3 de mayo de 1989.

[5] Simone Weil. "La personne et le sacré," in *Ecrits de Londres et dernières lettres* (París: Gallimard, 1957) 36.

[6] Alessandro Dal Lago. "La ética de la debilidad y el nihilismo," in *El pensamiento débil*, eds. Gianni Vattimo and Pier Aldo Rovanti (Madrid: Cátedra, 1980) 132.

[7] See Nelly Vialaneix. *Écoute Kierkegaard: Essai sur la communication de la parole* (París: Du Cerf, 1979) 102 ff.

[8] Leszek Kolakowski. "El sacerdote y el bufón," in *El hombre sin alternativa* (Madrid: Alianza Editorial, 1970) 316.

[9] *Ibid.*

[10] For Philo, who expressed Platonic ideas, "seeing" is the plenitude of knowledge, and Jacob's ears must have been changed into eyes, thus making him "a seer" after his struggle with the angel. Every Western philosophy and theology must have been accordingly formed by "eyes": the speculation that would reveal its entire pathology in the Hegelian system, according to Kierkegaard, in which eyes are, in addition, the representative sense of the aesthetic level of living.

The knowledge of reality only could be obtained through "the ear," the narration, the "whisper"; and the ethical level of living and later the religious level would be joined to them (Hans Jonas, "Heidegger et la théologie," *Esprit*, no. 140-141, July-August, 1988: 173-75, and N. Vialaneix, *op. cit.*, 204ff).

[11] *Op. cit.*

[12] Manuel Reyes Mate. "La memoria como ruptura." Speech presented at the VIHP seminar "La recuperación de la memoria histórica en el pensamiento espacial contemporáneo," directed by J. Nuguerza. Palacio de la Magdalena, Santander, 10-14 of July, 1989.

[13] Plato, *Phaedra*.

[14] Manuel Reyes Mate, *op. cit.*

[15] *Ibid.*

[16] *Ibid.*

[17] I. Benda. *La Trahison des clercs* (París, 1972), cited by Edward Timms, "Traición de los intelectuales? Benda, Benn y Brecht," *Debats*, no. 26 (Valencia Ediciones Alfonso el Magnanimo, 1988) 19.

[18] Nahum M. Sarna. *Exploring Exodus: The Heritage of Biblical Israel* (New York: Schocken Books, 1986) 25.

[19] Herbert Marcuse, cited in *Eros y Civilización*: "Artistic imagination gives form to the unconscious memory of freedom which failed because of the betrayed promise" (Barcelona: 1970) 140.

[20] José Ortega y Gasset, *Velázquez* (Madrid: Aguilar, 1987) 52.

[21] J. Jiménez Lozano, *Los ojos del icono* (Valladolid: Caja de Ahorros de Salamanca, 1988) 92-93.

[22] *Lucas* 38, 42.

[23] J. Ortega y Gasset, *op cit.*, 50.

[24] *Ibid.*, 59.

[25] Jonathan Brown. Sobre el significado de *Las Meninas*" in *Imágenes e ideas en la pintura española del siglo XVII* (Madrid: Alianza Editorial. 1985) 115.

[26] Simone Weil. *op. cit.* 30-31.

[27] *Ibid.* 31.

[28] Michel de Certeau. *La fable mystique* (París: Gallimard 1982) 62.

[29] Simone Weil, *op. cit.*, 37.

[30] J. B. Metz, *op. cit.*, 205: "The cognitive beginning of narrated remembrance leads philosophy to the critique of those forms of historical reason which more and more are reduced to a technology turned backward.... Within this technology of history the interest in liberty cannot even be an issue." And also: "What is new, that which has never existed, can

only be represented or brought into existence through narration. One reason that prevents the narrative interchange of the experiences of what is new or causes its rejection on account of its analytical nature and its autonomy, disappears in the task of reconstruction and is reduced ultimately to a technical function as Th. W. Adorno notes in the final passages of his *Mínima moralia* (206 and 215). And anyone can confirm this when faced with the dogmatic avalanche of technical studies of literature devoted to the craft of literature and a preoccupation with the technique of writers, which irritated Faulkner who wrote "If the writer is interested in technique, he should take up surgery or be a bricklayer." (William Faulkner to Jean Stein Vandem Heuvel, in *El oficio de escritor* (Mexico: Era, 1968) 174.

[31] Simone Weil, *op. cit.* 31.

[32] In reality, the miracle is peculiar to narration. W. Benjamin says that "the narrator takes what he tells from his own experience and that of others. And he converts it into the experience of those who listen to his story." J. Metz uses other words and a story by Martin Buber in expressing his comments on narration: "Narration is a happening, it has the function of a sacred act. . . . They once asked a rabbi, whose grandfather had been a disciple of Baal Shem Tov, to tell a story. . . . He said 'a story must be told in such a way that it provides a solution.' And he said the following: 'My uncle was a paralytic. They once asked him to tell a story about his teacher. Then he told how the saintly Baal Shem Tov used to jump and dance during prayer. My grandfather stood up and continued his narration which so enraptured him that he felt himself obligated to show, by jumping and dancing, how his teacher had done it. From that time on he was cured. That's the way stories must be told'" (in J. B. Metz, *op. cit.*, 215-16).

Julian Green writes that "Melville narrated his adventures to perfection, and the Hawthornes did not tire in listening to him. One day, in the course of a visit, he described a horrible battle which he had seen waged among savages on an island of the Pacific. One of the combattants performed marvellous feats of valor with an enormous club. He rained blows right and left, he crushed the enemy ranks with this terrible weapon. Nathaniel and Sophie listened to this story with their mouths open, without missing a word, a gesture. When Melville left, Hawthorne and his wife exchanged a thousand thoughts. 'Where is the club?' asked Mrs. Hawthorne suddenly. Hawthorne was persuaded that Melville had taken it with him and Mrs. Hawthorne held the opinion that he doubtlessly had put it in some corner. They looked for it." (J. Green, "Nathaniel Hawthorne: A Puritan, Man of Letters, 1804-1864," in *English Suite* (Madrid: Taurus, 1971) 167-68.

[Translation of an unpublished paper requested by the editor.]

JOSE CARLOS MAINER

José Carlos Mainer was born in Zaragoza in 1944. He has been professor of Spanish literature at the University of Barcelona and since 1982 at the University of Zaragoza. He has concentrated on Spanish literature of the nineteenth and twentieth centuries. Mainer has published many articles in literary magazines and newspapers. In his early years, he was interested in what he calls "sociology of literature," which is reflected in the book *Falange y literatura (Falange and Literature)* [1971]. He has subsequently dropped the word sociology in characterizing his writings and defines them as "histories of literature." He is concerned with Spanish society and culture as we see in his best-known work, *La edad de plata (1902-1939): Ensayo de interpretación de un proceso cultural (The Age of Silver (1902-1939): Interpretative Essay of a Cultural Process)*, which has had five editions since its original publication in 1975. A sequel to this book is *La doma de la Quimera: Ensayos sobre nacionalismo y cultura in España (The Taming of the Chimera: Essays on Nationalism and Culture in Spain)* [1988].

LITERATURE IN THE NEW DEMOCRATIC SOCIETY

From Mariano José de Larra until today to speak of the public in Spain involves a fundamentally moral and political problem. It has to do with trying to establish a peculiar form of ethics in writing, with wanting to forge an ideal alliance with someone who no longer exists (and with whom, in the forging of this alliance, the writer tends to shape the image of his desires and his frustrations). By virtue of assigning to the written word an added value, the writer begins to lose artistic autonomy in favor of reliance on other goals which are not always worthy of recommendation. To speak of the public in Spain is to think of Unamuno in his tenacious monologue with a believable Spaniard who is made out to be religious and doubting, mystical and supportive, misoneist and permeable. Or it is to speak of Antonio Machado and his poetic silence, or the gnostic road which he had his apocryphal characters explore. I wrote the following sometime ago, all the while conscious of being one more among those who had already said this and regretted his very words: for Spanish literature, as long as it is thought of as a public phenomenon, takes upon itself a political surplus given that its forms of expression are not always clear or viable, and that it invests itself with a condition that is highly perceptive of the national essence at a juncture where nationalism is experienced at an angle of collective tension.

Do these problems continue after 1975 within the scope of a crisis of values so unavoidably universal in magnitude, arising at a time when per capita income surpasses $3,000? Would it not seem at first glance that this could quite possibly be easily granted or that it could be emphatically denied. Political life recovered its credentials during the years of transition and this was what surely determined the eradication of that which was the most politicized aspect of literary and artistic life: authors who sang their own works, symbols of a meditative identity assumed with a guitar and a lot of collective responsibility, that, with some exceptions, contributed to prove the rule more than anything else. The last remnants of committed "authorsingers" [the term Mainer uses is *cantautores* which designates politicized performers who sang their own pieces to the audience] became silent and their publications even disappeared. *Triunfo* and *Cuadernos para el Diálogo* were among the best known of their publications, those which should be counted among the ones that at one time were the spiritual nutrients of a couple of repressed generations. An insolent and clumsy literature in favor of the buried régime, it would and did not endure for any length of time. This brazen literature tried to emulate the controversial glories of the pitiful cabaret theater of Muñoz Seca in the republican period, as well as the successes of Fernando Vizcaino Casa's novels which have disappeared from the bookstalls or have greatly diminished in importance. They were replaced--with more cleverness and a little bit of hypocrisy--by the empty words of Alfonso Ussía and the poisoned sophisms of that "master of journalists," Emilio Romero.

Perhaps the most evident clues of how that political lift has worn with time is detected in the profuse appearance of the theme of the Civil War in narrative and, above all, in the memoirs or remembrances of most anyone who has transcended anonymity: almost always mere personal viewpoints which ooze anecdotes, bile and concealments. Of an altogether different ilk, but less frequent in number, are the memoirs that have as a point of departure a more weighty intellectual and national experience. These are the ones whose authors are Dionisio Ridruejo and Pedro Laín Entralgo, Federico Sopeña, Jesús Aguirre and Eugenio Vegas as well as Julián Marías, Carlos Barral, Juan Gil-Albert and Francisco Ayala which provide--despite the unevenness of their aesthetic worth and the degree of sympathy we may have for these writers--general testimony and thoughtful reasons to convince us that Spanish democracy has been worthwhile. And that democracy has not been a fortuitous historical gift but rather the slow culmination of a conscious effort. The fact that the public has read these memoirs, although they have not always been the subject of the reasoned discussions that should have been devoted to them, seems to reveal that all attempts at writing memoirs are essentially outlets that transcend the individual authors. Since three of these memoirs--those of Ayala, Gil-Albert and Barral--have won very important prizes, it is evident that this genre of writing has been established aesthetically. Gil-Albert's memoir is an emotionally charged long monologue; Ayala's embodies precise and rationalistic testimony; and Barral's reflects a mood that swings between indifference and passion. They are each in their own right, the best examples of the best literary accomplishments in the genre in the past 15 years.

National Reverberations

But if literature seems to have clarified its contacts with active politics, the same cannot be said regarding the exploration of the nation's essence, a topic under which Spaniards boldly encompass many of their other problems. The Catalan case can be very notable with respect to how the cancer of linguistic polemics and the reverberations of a nationalism on the defensive can hinder the relationship of a literature with its natural public, when the two excellent works *Dietaris* by Pere Geimferrer and the memoirs of Antoni Tàpies and Josep María Castellet precisely reflect the coherence of a program of Catalan expression and the progressive involvement of a public. And, nevertheless, there still resounds that conclusion of the Congress of Catalan Culture which denied the condition of "Catalan writers" to anyone who wrote in Spanish, which by extension would designate as foreign such works as *Antagonía* by Luis Goytisolo, Juan Marsé's novels or the detective novels of Manuel Vázquez Montalbán, let alone Carlos

Barral's writings or the narrations of Eduardo Mendoza and the poems of José Agustín Goytisolo. It is clear that this "foreignness" has not harmed in any way the diffusion of these works and probably--as Georg Steiner pointed out some time ago--the same awareness of the conflict has enormously enriched the value of such texts. The problem is different. How can one deny Barcelona's representation in the elegiac, hard and tender adventures which Juan Marsé threads in that world bounded by the worker's district of Gracia and the bare hills of Carmelo? How can we fail to see in the entertaining "black novels" of Vázquez Montalbán the settling of accounts of an incorruptible critic in face of a communist crisis, a speculation concerning the magnitude of things as they were before they became what they are nowadays in Spain and the world at large, or even up until the formulation of that gastronomic neohedonism which has hued with pink-colored sauces and old-vintage wine from select cellars the problems of transition? And in the case of *Antagonía*, how can one not confer on the vast cyclical narrative of Luis Goytisolo the primacy that we would be hard put to spell out in its entirety and that the fine literary critic Gonzalo Sobejano opportunely called "recaptured memory," even when taken into account such competitors to that primacy of the order of José María Guelbenzu and José María Merino?

The case of a Barcelona which, despite so many things, refuses to be the cultural co-capital of the entire country is not a unique case. With the tragic background of an armed "fundamentalism," the Basque Country also transfers many of its historical or economic frustrations to its zeal in protecting its national identity. Several historical events have brought a confused state of turmoil to the Basques: the French Revolution and the war over the establishment of a constitutional government [in the early part of the 19th century], the atrocious Carlist wars, the Civil War (1936-39) and the decline of its industrial hegemony. An exceptional sculptor, Jorge Oteiza, after having stirred up a gloomy return to ethnic irrationality (in his passionate books: *Quosque tandem...!* and *Ejercicios espirituales en un túnel* (*Spiritual Exercises in a Tunnel*), accuses the current Basque government of cultural incapacity and, at the same time, he rejects the generous recognition of a national prize though he does not argue that his work represents "Spanish art." Like Gabriel Aresti (died 1975) and Blas de Otero (Otero also died before this piece was written) he hates Bilbao, but in his case, it is in the name of a rural and innocent ethnocentrism which he himself, being a Basque by heritage and political affiliation, could not easily take part in. It happens that Otero's aversion to the "model" city was resolved in a profound piety--which shines forth in the verses of his heir Jon Juaristi--whereas the imprecations of this great Basque author lead directly to that confused millennial spirit which feeds off his own moral misery.

What Remains of Spain

Naturally, the rest of Spain does not live its historical self-perception so dramatically. It is true that in 1978 Federico Jiménez Losantos published--and not without dearth of scandal--a book entitled *Lo que queda de España* (*What Remains of Spain*), which under the intellectual advocacy of Manuel Azaña, implicitly called for the edification of a secular, Spanish and liberal nationalism at a time when every one's ears were castigated by the ever present chantings of "Spanish State" and the Constitution itself opted for treading the middle road with the slogan "Castilian or Spanish language." But of significantly more weight in this matter are the serious works of José Luis Abellán, who has devoted himself since then to his *History of Spanish Thought*, in which he shows himself active in "recovering" the past dealing with Spanish exile (6 volumes from 1976 to 1987) or more recently, with the emigré thinkers in their encounter with Spanish-speaking America. That definitely can be called piously fulfilling a debt of honor and intelligence with the past. So many other acts of this sort have been accomplished that some times one wonders whether writers and their readers were so zealous in restoring the past because of a lack of any thought about how to write concerning the present. And there may be opportunistic reasons why there is a repetitious litany of 50 and 100 year-old celebrations, concerning the encounter of readers and authors. Especially since many of those homages have been implicitly more quiet, more reflective, more content to live the art and to bring together ethics and aesthetics, as exemplified by the centenaries of Juan Ramón Jiménez, Ortega and Manuel Azaña, all of which so eloquently speak of those who pursued the calling of beauty, vital passion and critical intelligence. Or I think of the continual pretexts to speak of the Generation of 1927, of the Residencia de Estudiantes and the Bohemian happiness of La Barraca, converted into a kind of collective adolescence that is secretly envied. Few things have contributed so much as these commemorations to reconcile a vast readership with another image of the country, with another way of perceiving ourselves.

Squandering of Public Resources

Not everything has gone well. Gratuitous vindications and pleas for spotting faulty merchandise have also abounded. And, of course, the ill-advised disinterment on the part of the neoregionalists, of less than convincing local glories that constitute the late flowering of what was called "recovery of the identity marks" which often have been in tune with the measurably diminished concepts of "popular culture" exhibited by city government representatives and provincial deputies. But it would also be unfair to judge by the same measure the whole of that copious bibliography. It is certain that it is easier today to publish a monograph on an unknown writer (which is suitable to the condition of "forgotten local glory") than to do so on Quevedo or on Lope de Vega. Consequently, the offices of county commissioners and of town halls are chock full of copies of never sold copies of facsimile editions, proceedings of erudite congresses, detailed studies on very insignificant topics and homages to those who are completely unknown. But despite so much waste of public resources and good paper, there are works which say much about the reorganization of university disciplines, more than short-lived literary magazines that were the ornament of some politicians who believed themselves patrons of the arts, and even books of writers who knew their trade. These publications are hidden away usually because of neglect rather than because of the indifference of a prospective readership. Could it be unthinkable that provincial Spanish publishers--and especially official institutions--might agree on some common and efficient means of distribution of their products? Could it not be feasible to establish a network of book stores--with public support--that specialize in reaching the many people interested in this kind of novelties, which oftentimes are harder to come by when published in the nearby autonomous region than when published in Shanghai or the Virgin Islands?

But the existence of a public interested in cultural events is the great novelty. It was born with democracy as though it were the explosion of pent up vitality. This new public patiently lines up in front of public museums, and on its own has gained the controversial free access to the museums. The new public has supported the flourishing of the opera and at its own cost has established a clever way to lower the price of the tickets for musical shows that are in demand. The new public has exhausted collections of book installments and books sold in kiosks. And this public deserves more than that lamentable role which some manipulators of political power assign to it and find praiseworthy, which is that of following a cult, of participating in merrymaking festivities aimed at promoting a cause. Who has said that to enjoy painting consists of personally smearing a canvas? Or that it is appropriate to set up "rockodromes," an atrocious sounding word, in order to scrape together some of the votes of young people completely lacking political enthusiasm? Who can hold the belief, if demagoguery does not counsel it, that culture consists of learning tawdry handicrafts, tormenting horned four-legged beings or donning outlandish garments and bellowing to ear-splitting sounds through electronic amplifiers? That perverse concept of "popular culture" which still is in vogue can effectively camouflage the many more substantial and overriding changes that the public's sensitivity has gone through in the last 15 years.

The moral changes of the Spanish people are much less irascible than one may think, much more stoic and even skeptical than what is recognized, and perhaps a tiny bit more disillusioned and passive than what necessity would have it during those 15 years. Spaniards' sensitivity has changed: it has acquired a more reverential sense of culture, it accepts more readily sentimental weaknesses, and it is more accommodating. Its taste, nevertheless, can still be marked by a certain tendency toward the indiscriminate and the rather simple, and the successes it has achieved bear a certain deleterious amount of sentimentality. I am thinking, to be sure, of certain stories of Miguel Delibes, e.g. *Los santos inocentes* (*The Innocent Saints*) and *El disputado voto del señor Cayo* (*The Disputed Vote of Mr. Cayo*), the popularity of Julio Llamazares' last novel, and of some imaginative works of Gonzalo Torrente Ballester, best sellers whose anatomy reveals some influence of the most common kind of emotionality. Perhaps this is why this sensitivity has led to the adoption of García Lorca as a kind of historico-literary fetish and to the acceptance of Antonio Gala as an oracle of its uncertainties. But I think that this tendency to become easily emotional can be due to growing pains which artists and those who manage art should give more attention to. Following the joy consequent upon first encounter, we ought to make increasing demands on ourselves because, in many respects, Spanish cultural life continues to abandon much that is desirable. We are still fonder of pretentious exhibitionism than of solid education. We bring great orchestras and the best directors to a country in which music conservatories are languishing. We erect splendid centers of art where we continue to commit outrages against the most elementary tenets of urban aesthetics, and where any corner is converted into a dump and where any white wall is covered with shameful inscriptions. We seek an excellent literature and prudent readers in a place where literary critics contribute little of themselves and the printed word of newspapers dangerously tilts toward irresponsibility and the gossip of those who have a messianic idea of their profession. The Spanish public is much more deserving of respect than what the politicians who court the public would have us believe or what the polls taken by "investigative journalism" say.

The public has accepted the fact that opinions must be plural. And this acceptance is seen in one of its favorite modalities as witnessed by the recently established radio phone-in show, which runs the danger of frequently magnifying anecdotes--someone has called this show "sociology"--where opponents are caricaturized, and where some people pontificate about things with which they hardly are acquainted and other people engage in shouting matches. These things are undesirable if what one desires is a form of pedagogy based on reasoned dialogue, though not one which would wear badly. As was pointed out before, we wonder whether it is the public which demands such phone-in radio shows and polls taken in the streets, or whether it is rather the laziness and little imagination of the radio reporters who put together these shows. The risk is to wind up thinking that a person with any notoriety who formulates an opinion shines scholarly each time a score is made through an ingenious turn of phrase, or that the broadsides of a person who has retired or the glibness of a politicized graduate student interviewed in the street about the students' strike or the contraceptive pill for men are representative of what people in general think. This though, is not "culture," but a mode of recreative anthropology. Though, again, there are opinions, and often they are well founded.

Public Opinion and the Press

Public opinion is voiced by the press especially so on occasions when the sales figures are still very far from their desired levels. There are newspaper columnists who write extremely well, have broad influence, and the repercussions of their writings are considerable. Their columns comprise the lively panorama of deception and hope, melancholy and the irritations of what we call the "transition." This has given Francisco Umbral his disposition, of combining cynicism and candor, and radicalism and politeness, which endows him with the ability to flatter a simple nymph of the jet society in the same way as he flatters Dolores Ibárruri. This shapes the solid, incorruptible morals of Manuel Vázquez Montalbán, or the Mediterranean skepticism of Manuel Vicent who, from time to time, issues tirades against the bull fight although he prefers to dream of real beaches of paradise anywhere in the world. This stimulates the furious diatribes of

Rosa Montero, the schemes of complicated prose and devastating irony of Rafael Sánchez Ferlosio, and the Socratic skill of Fernando Savater. The list would be interminable and almost leads us to the conclusion that the newspaper article is the topical formula of a cast of thought that circumstances make capital of in short evasive pieces, in rapid notations, in the discourses of perplexing opinion. There is a lot of this among the new columnists, and it is pertinent to surmise that this holds true among their readers. And one might also conjecture that the latter constitute a middle class that is quite numerous, more progressive in morals than in politics, more cautious than soul-searching, more hedonist than generous. The public which grew out of this one, rooted as the former in the middle class, is less numerous. It is not that expanding mid-cult public which has forged the patronage of democracy in a country where there was only bread and soccer, but the heir of that other privileged public which joined in political protest and hungered for culture in the ominous years of the Franco era.

It is very easy to accuse the public--and we have almost done so--of being acquiescent and of being dazzled with excessive naiveté by the new light shining forth from democracy. Of course, it leans toward a certain affectation and its favorite reading material or contemplative pastime often have a tinge of sentimental overindulgence. It is as if its senses were dulled and it needed a certain bunghole for its higher-pitched feeling to appreciate better what actually comes their way. Perhaps for this reason these new readers have found ideally suited to their emotional tempo the droopy and baggy clothes with bright colors and indolently curved forms. For them, Juan José Millás organizes the geometry of his novels, Soledad Puértolas develops light relationships in her narrations, and Antonio Muñoz Molina designs his complex musical plots.

But this is not the moment to delve into contemporary customs and manners. In the area of literary consumption, vogues pass on with comforting rapidity. Literature not only explores the most visible and ostentatious horizons of people's lives but it also investigates the deepest feelings and less conscious strata for these are also the image of life. It has to do with the fact that freedom has already authorized all possible explorations. And what clearly comes from this is that literature has found its public. As a result, the normalization of literary society has come upon us, most certainly at least upon one of the estimations made at the beginning of this essay. It is clear that when we deal with literature and its readership in our country, it will still continue to be tantamount to making a moral and political statement, though one that will no longer pave our way to a dismal prison cell, to the surrounding severities of judicial confinement or to a gravestone marking the spot where we lay. After the end of the Franco era, there did not come into existence--a fact which many people noticed--a new golden age that was kept hidden away in the writers' drawers, although no one can vouch against the fact that we are living in an exciting and rich age of Spanish letters. What appears, and would that it be everlasting, is the reconciliation of literature with its abiding condition of freedom, enlightenment and spirit of togetherness.

The Lack of Learning Culture in the Schools

In conclusion, what is lacking--although amounting to a lot--can be made more easily available. Culture is sorely lacking and the teaching of culture in the schools is the only possible support for more assiduous reading. It happens, nevertheless, that teaching programs, dazzled by the nomenclature of modern linguistics, are miserly in their teaching of literature and that a certain prejudice of modern pedagogues in favor of "personal experimentation" and of that which is utilitarian, has cast into oblivion collective readings, the teaching of literary history, the assiduous practice of writing and the study of grammar along more imaginative lines, all of which are the best means to approach reading. There ought to be no disregard for the disadvantageous competition and distractions which these initiatives will encounter in this age and time through the fascination with visual image and loud-sounding music. There is also missing a more active cultural policy in favor of reading, although this presupposes taking away funds from those glittering activities which have often been the object of serious criticism. All of this means greater financial outlay for books, the establishment of more generous funds for the promotion of public libraries, and even making forthcoming greater effort to see to it that books are sent to rural areas. Finally, there is the need for a more constructive criticism, that is less arbitrary, less preoccupied with fads and more in tune with its pedagogical mission, less improvised and more professional, even at the cost of seeing superficial brilliance emptied of its aggressiveness and snob appeal.

[Translation of an essay published in *Cuenta y razón* 48-49 (July-August, 1989) 35-42]

XAVIER RUBERT DE VENTOS

Xavier Rubert de Ventós was born in Barcelona in 1939. He studied law at the University of Barcelona and later went to the University of Madrid where he received his doctorate in philosophy in 1964. He is currently professor of Aesthetics at the University of Barcelona. Rubert de Ventós was a member of the Spanish Parliament and is an elected member of the European Parliament. He was a visiting professor at the University of Cincinnati (1964), a Santayana Fellow at Harvard University (1972), a visiting scholar in the Faculty of Architecture, University of California, Berkeley (1973), and has taught at the Universities of Mexico and Caracas. He has written on aesthetics, philosophy, culture, history, and ethics. Among the more than twelve books he has written in Spanish and Catalan, the two that stand out are *El laberinto de la hispanidad (The Hispanic Labyrinth)* [1987], which deals with Spanish culture and the relationship between Spain and Latin America in the last five centuries; and *De la modernidad: Ensayo de filosofía crítica (On Modernity: A Critical Philosophical Essay)* [1980], a keen analysis of modernism and postmodernism.

FROM NATIONALISM TO NUCLEARISM

In World War I some 15 million people died and about 50 million in World War II. One must expect then that technological and logistic sophistication would have a much more devastating effect in the event of a third world war, even if atomic weapons are not used. It would then stand to reason that the danger of a new conflagration would not arise so much from nuclear weapons as it would from those very reasons that brought about the two previous ones: 1) nationalism camouflaged by universalism, universalism of race, of class or what have you; and 2) the claim of establishing a mistaken political status quo out of a military one, as came about in the wake of the Versailles and Yalta treaties.

Rather than forget recent history and use the nuclear factor as a scapegoat for all the evils and dangers awaiting us, it is fitting to pay attention to the positive or negative effect which the substitution of conventional weapons for nuclear ones may have on war-causing eventualities. The least we can say about such eventualities is that they are ambivalent. If, on one hand, there is no doubt that Hiroshima came to reinforce and to petrify post-war status sanctioned in Yalta, on the other hand, this strengthening has wound up weakening the legitimacy and meaning of the first of those causes: the universal nationalism of the modern State based on a curious mixture of warlike poetics, ideological rhetoric, and protectionist prose.

Indeed, the display of force and power which nuclear balance requires, as Glucksman has shown, lies in the "visibility" of power, in its pure and harsh manifestations. For did not Kant point out that the guarantee of universal peace is precisely this publicity of intention--the end of a "secret state" within which war preparations were being hatched? In a way different from what held true in previous wars, the ones who have to verify weapons in this day and age are the enemies, and these weapons must be hidden or camouflaged from neighbors fearful of the closeness of nuclear arms which may qualify them as targets. But this very need to show weapons to the enemy, added to the magnitude of their potential effects, is what has transformed nuclear conflict into the "pure and impossible" form of war understood as a confrontation which may beget the triumph of one of the parties. If something makes this "impossible war" imaginable, even likely or probable, it is not the installation of nuclear missiles, but, on the contrary, the proliferation of conventional arms not permitting the immediate recourse to nuclear weapons nor the creation of nuclear havens that would arguably give latitude to entertain the thought of survivability.

The monotheism of atomic deterrence thus paves the way for the crisis of polytheism based on the creed of nationalistic persuasion. Now we are all pawns and subjects of this new monotheism of terror. This holds true for *each one of us*, since unlike the classic weapons which permitted a distinction (one which was at least theoretical) between the front and the rear guard, between the military and civilians, with the new bomb there is no longer any distinction drawn between economic and racial disparities. All of us are hostages on equal footing to the bomb, which throws together the mechanism and effects of nuclear dissuasion with those of terrorism according to Baudrillard. Since 1945 we have all discovered the priority collective death has over being killed off individually; we have come to know that extinction awaits us as a species. This possibility can become a reality if we continue along the road leading nation-states to act the part of nation-states, whereby the complicity of passion and reason dictates the present modes of containment against aggression.

But how much stress can these modes of containment face up to? The old nations certainly appear to be more and more ineffective and obsolete from the time when international corporations drained them of their economic clout and the new world correlation of forces established limits to their military independence and their ideological viability. But one must not forget the good health still enjoyed by nationalism and its capacity to strengthen itself by the very paradoxical fact of having attained its clearest "level of incompetence." International corporations, with their computer science and their television series, pervert the national sense of purpose, and end up strengthening it by concentrating on the sale of computers, a fact which permit a foolproof measure of internal control and ushers in the necessity of acquiring combat vehicles in order to strengthen the external position of each state. The international corporation of atomic terror, which by virtue of its own intermediacy should break the nationalistic discourse, finally ends up also serving it to support and reassert through it, as in France, its neocolonial position. ("Our force of dissuasion is demonstrating its efficiency in Africa without any need of using it," states Deleuze. In rejecting it, as in Germany, the foundation is laid for materializing the hope of national re-unification.

Christian Nationalism

But what was and still is the reason for the modern State? Let us see. The reason for family ties is kinship, for a guild it is a professional one, for a church it is spiritual, and for a State it is territorial. The reason for a State's existence is diametrically opposite to the others. When compared to the intimate and personal nature of family ties, of the clan and of the church, the State offers from the start a relationship of only spatial contiguity or territorial unity. Consequently, neither the internal expansion (codification of laws) nor the external one (colonization) of the Roman State could claim any kind of personal conviction. Roman law did not require anyone to be good, but to be as bad as the regulations allowed. The empire did not demand that the conquered peoples accept Roman gods, brought instead the conquered gods (Demeter, Isis, Castor) to their own abiding culture and gave them a place alongside their own deities.

This respect and tolerance, which belongs to strictly territorial relationships, is shattered when the new Christian State finds a spiritual reason--not merely a spatial one--for its consolidation and expansion. Thereafter, every nationalism will have to legitimize its expansive aspirations through universalist ideals: thus has tradition been fashioned after the consecration of Christianity, of socialism, of "the guarantee of freedom, civilization and common heritage" (according to the preamble of NATO), and so forth. Marx was the first to denounce the modern secular State as the perfect realization of the Christian-made confessional State, though by his own admission the former has fallen short of supremacy over the latter. And his disciples are the ones who have taken it upon themselves to give us the last practical example of this in converting Marxism-Leninism into the rhetoric and liturgy of Russian imperialism.

The force and inertia of this idealized patriotism or territorialism did not end, indeed, in the galvanization and confrontation of European states. The very logic of Christian nationalism crystallizing into Protestant nation-states, has, in the aftermath of the two European civil wars, led to the satellization of a Europe which is beginning to be considered as merely tactical factor--i.e., instrumental or negotiable--in the game of balance of power and nuclear dissuasion. If matters keep to this course, not only Europe but all humanity can end up being a tactical hostage to a nuclear strategy, based on the convictions that their "souls"--as those of witches according to the theory of St. Thomas--can be saved through their own holocaust. This is a new version, of the commonplace saying to the effect that "the operation was a success, but the patient died."

From all of which there follows that the nuclearization of the world and the monopoly of its arsenal held by the Bolshevik and the American imperialisms, epitomizes the immediate cause of this situation and is both the logical result and the culmination of the nationalism which Christian universalism territorialized, and which thus established the impious alliance between Territory and Reason, between Space and Truth. In their holy war to determine whether they are hound-dogs or the sort that can boast of pedigree, European nationalisms have wound up allowing power to escape toward its periphery, toward Eurasia and North America. And thus it came about that the national explosion of that dangerous amalgam gave way, or, if you will, passed the torch to those bearers who hold in store for the world a new era of imperialist deep-freeze.

Pagan Imperialism

The political reality of our time is no longer national but imperialist. As far as European nationalism is concerned, to refuse to acknowledge this situation is to resign oneself to being a passive subject of the situation and to accept it without taking the trouble to give it thought. The only sensible thing is to wonder what role European countries want to play in this arrangement. Are they trying to constitute themselves into a "third empire" or into an appendage of an empire? But the attitude most resorted to continues to be the denunciation of this imperialism and its dangers, and striving to legitimize nationalism as the only force of containment against imperialism. Nationalism will assure responsibility for "freedom" of those nations over which it holds sway. What would independent Corsica, Alsace and the Canary Islands be short of nothing else, but appendages of Washington? The truth, nevertheless is that such nationalism is not only possible or viable but rarely is it useful or desirable. Let us then be guided by our ultimate concern and look at its impossibility or undesirability.

Impossibility, first of all, to happily continue to cultivate these topological nationalisms which were understood to be carriers of the universal Torch of the Spirit from whose flame minds took heed and set about to purify the entire world. Today, the nuclearization of politics *obliges* us to reject this attitude, but all the while, providing a helping hand to do so. The evidence that the world is divided along the lines of seeking out an equilibrium of power or a purely military dissuasion obviously drains any pact or bloc of any universalist or theoretical legitimacy. Rumania, Hungary, East Germany and Czechoslovakia do not only resist being not only "Communist," but also, since the installation of the SS 20, they resist being privileged targets. Ideological persuasion yields to crude and hard military dissuasion. Ideological legitimacy can nowadays only survive in those states in which Christianity did not become secularized and was transformed into nationalist politics; but where it rather continues to be the last and explicit rationale for the existence of a country (Poland) or resistance (Ireland) of a people. What in any event causes the breakdown of the credibility and legitimacy of the curious mixture of pagan localism and Christian universalism which is found at the base of modern nationalism, and the military caste charged ex officio with its maintenance, and with the series of holocausts it has spawned.

An atomic holocaust nonetheless has sufficed to exhaust the rationale of any of the would-be rationales pretending to become founts of inspiration for the advent of other holocausts, and have thus caused a crisis in the particular ethos, constituting the nationalistic foundation of the dominant States. Their wide-spread power to blackmail and destroy has made impossible the universality of their justification and has in actuality made us lapse back into the groundwork of a state analogous to that which characterized the Roman states as an imperialism without ethics. Is this situation more undesirable than the previous one? Prior to the holy alliance between the realm of the spatial and that of the ideal, which has set the stage for modern nationalism, territorial expansion had been purely normative or legal as it was in Rome, or strictly a risky enterprise as in medieval Christianity. Considering the essence of Christianity's subjective ambiance of piety, exterior activity seemed to be an uncertain undertaking:

akin to the non-essential plateau of conquests and sagas. Whether it is because each locale or terrain has its pagan god or because God lies more in the beyond or in the here and now of our earthly bounds, neither Christian feudalism nor Roman imperialism ever brought forth this topological and expansionist hybrid, the nation-State, or for that matter, that universal construct of Hegel's systematically pursuing the policy (in accordance with Céline's reading of Hegel's idea of the state, having to do with exploiting its citizens, and rearing them for the espousing and the upholding of a cause). Since one must not forget that the most dangerous reaction and expansive wave is the one sprung from the encounter between the commonplace and the logical, a "national reaction" which only today begins to appear neutralized by the "atomic reaction." In any case it is clear that in a nuclear context, that expansive nationalism is no longer feasible among secondary states and turns out to be less and less capable of ideological legitimation in imperialist states, given the increasing evidence of the pure system of forces on which it is based.

It is therefore fitting to imagine for the near future a deflation of national ideology and its erosion from both extremes: from below (i.e., from the people) or from above (i.e., from the empires). One must bear in mind that an alliance strengthened by a natural tendency to make way for entente among groups, countries, classes or generations that are not contiguous: aristocrats and peasants, uncles and grandchildren, or as the case may be. Moreover, there will be a crisis of that ideology from within: from a capillary nationalism, which at the same time protects people from lawlessness and vaccinates them against the eruption of new messianic nationalisms. It is also a crisis from without: emerging from an Empire which could end up like the Roman one, seduced by its own conquests and more concerned with what was happening on its periphery than what was taking place at is very core.

A case in point illustrating the limits which have been reached, is that of a policeman I encountered in Tijuana whose job it was to prevent the illegal entry of Mexicans into the United States. He said to me: "Look here, Americans are those very people who sneaked in before, as those who now infiltrate the border will in time come to be." I then imagined the possibility of a country that is constituted at any given moment, not by a race or by a universal class, but only by those who "sneaked in" earlier. If a country with an imperialistic bent of mind, more topical than actual, leaves itself open to the infiltration of outside elements much as it became the lot of Rome to experience to the fullest, could it not come to reproduce the pure, loose form of the Empire?

It was only a figment of the imagination, of mine at any rate. Or rather perhaps an incapacity for imagining much more. Or even perhaps, by dint of stretching the point a bit further beyond these extremes, it was the proclivity of the human mind of placing itself on the side of the evil that wells up in us when we do not have the strength or courage to come to grips with it.

[Translation of an essay taken from *Europa y otros ensayos (Europe and Other Essays),* 1986]

IMBROGLIO AND DEVELOPMENT

The Spaniards did not throw themselves into the simple and lineal "development" of America precisely because they began by letting themselves be embroiled in and seduced by the new world. It would undoubtedly have been more practical and efficient not to allow themselves to be wrapped up in this identity crisis but to view America and its inhabitants as the tabula rasa from which they could further their interests, plan the fulfillment of their ideals, establish their feudal estates and raise their families. It seemed that this was going to be the case when they imposed on the new virgin territory the medieval social structure of the *encomienda* [large land holdings granted to settlers], the concept of the cities that came about in the Renaissance, the toponymic analogies of the Iberian Peninsula, and even their own myths and legends. But the truth of the matter is that the Spaniards soon deliberately began to crossbreed with the natives--the new laws made all rights applicable to the half-breeds and from 1503 on mixed marriages were encouraged--and also began to question the legitimacy of the conquest, to defend theologically the freedom and equality of the Indians, to learn their language and to marvel at their cultural diversity.

This is not the case of Anglo-Saxon colonization. Hegel wrote in 1820 that "in South America and Mexico, the inhabitants who had feelings of independence were the *criollos*, those born in the New World. On the other hand, the English pursued in the Indies the policy of preventing the crossbreeding of Indians and Europeans, whose offspring would feel love for their own country."[1] Hegel attributed Anglo-Saxon behavior to tactical reasons, as writers who have tried to explain the Spaniards' behavior have done at different times. Unlike the "founding fathers" [of the United States], the "Conquistadors travelled alone, which led them to intermingle with the Indian women, and unlike the Anglo-Saxons, who came across nomadic tribes considered to be barbaric (e.g. the *chichemecas*) by the natives themselves, the Spaniards encouraged highly developed empires like those of the Incas and Aztecs."

But none of these reasons can sufficiently explain what is a more complex and profound cultural difference. Could it be that the Anglo-Saxons began to see what was happening with nationalism arising in South America from the close association of peoples born of Spanish stock and the *mestizo* elements, and for this reason they opted for implementing means of extinction, or the concentration of Indians on reservations? Did not the Jesuits defend the savages of the Orinoco or of the Casanares plains as much or more than Las Casas did the inhabitants of the Aztec empire? And did this not have something to do with the paradoxical fact that the rational and systematic behavior which explains a rapid and efficient conquest did *not* translate in later centuries into a modernization of the Spanish colonies parallel to that of the Anglo-Saxons?

Cortez's capacity to manipulate myths, to exploit discord, to use the language (of the natives), to usurp symbols and take advantage of the superstitions of the Aztecs is without doubt one of the most spectacular examples of this "astute vivacity and worldly science"--the description is that of his enemy Las Casas--which characterizes the modern temper of Renaissance Europe. Contrary to the holistic and magical temper of the Aztecs, that of Cortez is characterized by an individualistic and lineal attitude which stems from a "disenchanted" conception of nature, which distinguishes between facts and values, subject and object, natural laws and social norms. This conception is that of a world which is a discrete and homogenous vast reality in which it is no longer a matter of participating but of understanding and controlling it. The success of this instrumental rationality vis-à-vis the indigenous organization and mentality was as rapid as it was spectacular. Arturo Uslar Pietri wrote that "in 50 years the whole continent was subjugated and surveyed; cities were formed; jurisdictions were established; laws, language and religion were put in place; schools were founded; institutions were organized; ports and roads were opened; and a common and permanent lifestyle was created... In 1528, books written by Boccaccio and Erasmus arrived at the island of Cabruga, on the Venezuelan coast, where a city with its church and government palace was built and in which municipal elections were held. A century later New York City was founded (1629) and it was more than 200 years later that Chicago was founded on the shores of Lake Michigan."

How is it then that this initial advantage did not materialize in the political and economic modernization of Latin America? I believe that this very speed was responsible for the later difficulties in their development.

1. On the one hand, the precociousness and efficacy with which those modern legal and administrative structures were imposed would later serve to halt the formation of new mercantile and liberal structures. In the animal world, this phenomenon is known as *neotaenia* or premature growth.

2. On the other hand, the speed with which the racial and cultural mixture was carried out does not permit a unidirectional assimilation, but rather the "modern culture" remains forever impregnated with the indigenous values and reflections which would be forever shaping it from within. We see it in the language, and one does not have to be very perspicacious to recognize that much of the institutionalized corruption of current Latin American administrations stems from a heroic resistance against those bureaucratic and impersonal relationships imposed from without by the workings of a culture trying to repersonalize them, even though this may negatively come about through the bribe [translator's note: the author uses the colloquial Mexican word *mordida* which literally means "bite"].

3. Finally, it is this easily accomplished success of the conquest which, through an adverse turn of events, was to strengthen the heroic spirit as opposed to industrialism, the search for booty or the imposition of tribute instead of rational exploitation, of attaining glory rather than earning profits, or the cultivation of verbal idealism always aimed at decreeing great principles (justice, liberty, etc.) as opposed to the far-sightedness and industriousness which characterized the development of Anglo-American countries.

The rapid Spanish conquest (in opposition to the slow Anglo-Saxon colonization) also had its perverse effects on the development of the Iberian Peninsula, an effect which turned out to be a truly "poisoned gift." This process is not new: the competition making expansion or growth possible turns out to be lethal when not changed to adapt to the new medium it generates. Fichte interpreted in a similar manner the crisis of the Hellenic city-state: Greek democracy conquered Persian despotism, but its own habits, more devoted to the city than to the state, led it to set up in Asia colonial cities which fought among themselves, weakening the metropolis and leaving it ripe for Roman domination. In an analogous way, Roman expansion and unification created the ideological bases and the vehicle for expansion of the new Christian religion, first the universal Pauline state (which still uses the structure of the Roman state to Christianize people "if only outwardly"), and later the Germanic states whose identity and independence took root, as had never happened previously, in the soil of Christianity "from which its own state arose."

In the case of Spain it happened that, as Max Weber put it, "colonial commerce did not stimulate work or technological development since it rested on a principle of plunder and not on a calculation of profitability based on market possibilities... Thus, the influx of precious metals to Spain supposes a parallel regression of the capitalistic system in this country. The flow of precious metals passed through Spain without hardly affecting it, and profited, on the other hand, those countries which from the 12th century on had been transforming their attitudes toward work, a circumstance which favored the beginnings of capitalism." And the circle was finally completed when America, which determined Spain's underdevelopment, wound up receiving underdeveloped influences from it.

Beyond this boomerang effect is the fact that Spain appeared again and again faced with "modernizing" cultural forces whose common denominator was the progressive independence of the civil urban society and the clear delimitation between temporal and spiritual matters. In the same year in which Cortez took Tenochtitlán, his individualistic spirit was defeated in Villalar. The Castilians expelled the Jews during Columbus' first voyage, tried to prevent through Queen Isabella's testament the participation of the Catalans, utilized the gold from America to fight against the Protestants and later had to defend their independence against the children of the Enlightenment. On all fronts they opposed the forces which prepared modern development through the disenchantment of the world and the complementary distillation of a Reason and Piety, a Virtue and an Interest, all of which were pure. The Jesuit experience in America was an heroic and a frustrated attempt to conquer this modernity without renouncing that frame of mind.

It is in opposition to the Catholic Church that the process of the disenchantment of reality required by the new system of production was to be carried forth and affirmed. Lutheran protestantism had the task of alienating the secular world from religious bonds and inertia, Calvinism continued giving a positive religious sanction to the money-making business of this world, and finally the Enlightenment took it upon itself to implement the replacement of old structures of legitimacy with new deities, those of Reason, Virtue, or Progress. And in the interim, Spain, while politically contending with all of this, proved herself incapable of making further headway anchored as she was in political precociousness which had at first held out the promise of being able to play a competitive role in modern industrial society. The first and most heroic attempt to make good this economic modernization, without going full circle in order to accomplish all its political and ideological implications was that of the Jesuits in Colombia, Paraguay and Uruguay; the very last--pathetic, true, though not sterile--was that of the Opus Dei during the sixties, brilliantly highlighted in one of its conclaves by Laureano López Rodó.

Lutheranism thus collaborated in the process of taking God out of the world, and of business, by introducing Him inside the individual. Intense piety had to take a firm stand and cast all its worldly forms into given molds until its devotees fell into place in a phalanx of *res extensa* ("heads of cattle"). As a result clocks took over Church bells, personal reading of the Bible became more important than sermons, and princes superseded popes. From then on it was the individual who seized the tremendous responsibility and blame before God--"You believe that you have escaped the cloisters but now you will be a monk for your whole life"--, which until that time had been wisely administered and exorcised with brief prayers and indulgences, homilies, and periodical devotions and confessions. The elimination of confession destroyed the "fifth column" which the Church counted on for the imposition of its criteria on the secular world, and there occurred the disappearance of the balance of power--to the benefit of the State--which until then had existed between the Church morality and reasons of state. The lax and confused dialectic of Sin-Repentance decreed by the Church was replaced by a clear and distinct delimitation of spheres: internal piety and political laws or external economic ones, individual austerity, and social pragmatism.

Lutheran protestantism had acted as the "antithesis" which separated both spheres, but it was left to Calvinism to establish the new "synthesis" in preaching the preestablished harmony between worldly success and eternal salvation. Separated by Luther, the lay virtue came to colonize the religious ones and to restore a new bourgeois universalism equally opposed to all the virtues of the state: action as opposed to monastic contemplation, sobriety as opposed to ecclesiastic and courtly ostentation, predestination in the other world and the desire for profit in this world as opposed to traditional freedom and the equality of men preached by the Church. This was an inversion of roles which would reach its zenith the day erastianism came to require that the dogma of incarnation or the existence of purgatory yield to the authority of Parliament.

NOTE

[1] Although Rubert de Ventós has many notes in his book, they are generally descriptive and do not provide appropriate bibliographical references for his citations. In this essay and the following one, the notes have been left out in order to present a smoother flow of ideas.

[Translation of an essay taken from *El laberinto de la hispanidad (The Hispanic Labyrinth)*, 1987].

ENCOUNTERS IN THE LABYRINTH

The Spanish experience is a model from which each person can select the orientation or inspiration which most suits one's fancy. As an example, Adam Michnik, the Pole who was the Director of KOR and Solidarity, specifically referred to Spain in his proposal for "a compromise between the pertinence of the Warsaw Pact and the transformation of political and social structures." He concluded by saying that "the Spanish model constitutes for us a great hope. Spain is a viable model to make the transition from dictatorship to democracy." There is no doubt that Michnik did not count on the fact that the Church was not going to be able to play the role there which the Monarchy played in our situation and that the USSR was not the United States.

In their own search to find a breakthrough to democracy, Latin American republics can profitably look to the Spanish monarchy's evolvement of constitutional norms, which meant successfully dealing with a lack of democratic tradition and consolidation. Latin America has no other recourse but to seek a principle or referent for building democracy based on such traditions as she has to accomplish this feat, immanent to her own social reality, and capable of transcending present-day political struggles, a principle that the American republics have to find on their own soil and in their own experience, in their tradition and their liturgies, and with which they can face this other tradition they inherited from their Spanish patrimony, a patrimony of coups and corruption which constitutes our most shameful legacy in America, and the true nature of the "black legend." It is, moreover, the very historical memory of the protective role of the Spanish monarchy, which even today remains alive in many indigenous communities, that can be made to act as an asset in the shared symbols or references the Latin American community ought to recuperate. By no means does this have to do with claiming any right of Spanish sovereignty over Latin America. Rather it concerns the opposite of this, the right which Latin Americans--as well as those people of Sephardic origin or from Gibraltar, or even those from regions of Spain seeking their independence--can claim of this monarchy to share in it with the Spaniards, and to use it eventually for their own ends or objectives. As soon as any Latin American fear or reticence is dispelled regarding the possibility of Spanish hegemony over them, there does not appear to be any reason why, as King Juan Carlos I has said, "linked as brethren by one language, by a common past and a singular conception of the world, we cannot seek together to resuscitate the importance and influence which the Hispanic people on both sides of the

Atlantic had."

On another level, which is more circumstantial, perhaps Latin America can follow that special path between voluntarism and empiricism, social democracy and populism, which Spanish democracy has taken. The courageous efforts of Adolfo Suárez and the tenacity of Fraga Iribarne and Carrillo, which proved capable of converting even the most reluctant to the side of democracy, gave way to the controlled boldness of Felipe González and a new generation of politicians and labor leaders, who for their own part proved themselves capable of going naturally from clandestine activities to the negotiating table, to play the democratic game for high stakes. They strictly adhered to the rules of the game in their efforts to achieve an efficient pact between the socialist dogma upheld by them and autonomous and professional economic interests indispensable if the country is to keep a dynamic course of action. It represented a break with the ingrained mind-set of corporate and patrimonial key directives. It is a mind-set which still has to come to terms with a university recently saturated with jobholders and with a party from which no alternatives were forthcoming. It was an economic and social liberalization which undertook the privatization of public enterprises and the deregulation of productive sectors, and which put its money, albeit with less audacity, on a pluralistic twist which came across well on television. It seemed that the pendulum which oscillated from dogmatic and messianic faith to passiveness or indifference had been put to rest. Finally, Ramiro de Maeztu's affirmation that "we have not been born here to be Kantians" was refuted.

This option was especially bold and opportune in a moment in which the prevailing tendency in the most advanced capitalist economies seemed to be oriented in an inverse sense: economic liberalism paradoxically and perversely allied to a new ideological and state fundamentalism. (In this climate, thus was privatization accredited and thus did it commit itself to argue on behalf of the public good that it had the moral right to apply and secure public concessions from the state; thereupon declarations were formulated to make known the faith placed in civil society and market economy, and in the English language as the official language of California, and in the mandatory practice of school prayers. All this came at a time when it seemed quite opportune to send a significant message to Latin American countries where the formation of capital and structures of production have always been mediatized by forms of government which have tried to be modernizing factors without being modern themselves, for rarely were these governments able to bring about either the coming into being or the development of middle classes, who are burdened with the direct responsibility for 67% of the foreign debt of these countries.

All this does not mean that a greater union and cooperation would have to come about on the basis of the influence of the Spanish process on Latin America. The struggles for liberation from Mexico to Nicaragua, the current political evolution of Brazil, Uruguay and Argentina and the efforts made at the Contadora meeting to arrive at a solution of problems besetting Central America are present-day examples for us. And much before this,

Spain will have to learn from the infinite skills displayed by these countries in assuming and going beyond the problematic tradition which we left them: to absorb, conserve and enrich the nature of their language, to assimilate the outpourings of Spanish sense of pride through the channels of their innate reserve, and to instill in them an exquisite graciousness, to transform the colonial complex into a new identity capable even of giving shelter to the intellectual élite which was subject to persecution in the "mother country," etc. A versatility which in Mexico produced the first synthesis between Anglo-Saxon pragmatism and Latin positivism ("the scientists"), the first popular revolution of the modern era and the original synthesis of vanguardism and the native elements found in its murals.

We saw that, with the new monarchy Spain seemed to initiate the recuperation of its traditionalism, being still in need to lose the remaining centralist traits which came about as a result of its national precociousness combined with its social poverty. It seems that with the socialists, Spain has recaptured the classical and neoscholastic ideal of a non-Calvinist modernization, and the only thing left for these Socialists is to finish a profound study of their task and pay their last tribute to the country. This last tribute can not be paid until they lose the elections and show in this way, as is fitting in a democratic country, that there is no ideology among us making claims to a unique path of salvation as a must, nor any eternal generation, nor any indispensable or charismatic option. But in the meantime, for the purpose of making clear to themselves their task, they may very well lay claim to have undoubtedly learned not only to be headstrong but porous; to recoup the traditional permeability of Spanish culture, not only the reflections of a more or less enlightened despotism. They will then have finally lost the mania of solidifying Spain and will discover that political homogeneity must be brought about inductively by society at large, not by state decree. Accordingly, along with economic liberalization they will need the liberalization of political parties and of the electoral system. Then they will cease to represent socialism as invincible in only one part of the whole, and leave behind them the pretension of being able to exercise government authority over "autonomies without autonomists," by virtue of recognizing their impotence to lord it over historical nationalities already constituted into a whole and industrialized, such as the Basque country and Catalonia.

* * * * *

Does Spain's colonial and present-day experience have something to reveal to North Americans? Apart from the "values" it may embody, does it have any orientation to offer? It is doubtlessly a symbol, but can it also operate as a guide?

Up to this point, we have seen rather the contrary. The private and sectarian nature of the colonization of the North culminated in the liberalism and dynamism of North American society, in contrast with the impotence and grandiloquence which Spanish American apologetic officialism frequently turns out to be. The religious principles which inspired the Founding Fathers were more propitious than the Church dogmas that gave rise to opportune pacts and compromises in important matters with bourgeois ethics. The latter code of ethics might be, as Ortega thought, "morally and vitally inferior to the integral solidarity" of dogmatic or war-like ethics, but it certainly is the case that it founded and is at the base of modern democracy, as well as of a looser and more effective imperial political system which is more spatial than moral, more economic than ideological.

This secularization of principles, which is necessary and effective, came about at a high price. We know too well its cruel practical effects and we also saw that in Europe that the old myths of divine or natural right were not eliminated but replaced by those of the State or Reason. In the United States this secularization did not take place without a process of historical amnesia and metaphoric impoverishment which has resulted in posing practical problems. The Spanish experience can be valid today not only as historical testimony but also as practical orientation.

[Translation of part of the last essay published in *El laberinto de la hispanidad (The Hispanic Labyrinth)*, 1987]

FERNANDO SAVATER

Fernando Savater was born in San Sebastián in 1947. He received his doctorate in philosophy from the University of Madrid. He held the chair of Ethics at the University of Madrid before assuming the same chair at the University of the Basque Country in 1982. He has been a visiting professor in the United States, Mexico, Argentina, Venezuela, Denmark, and Italy. Savater has written more than forty books: collections of essays on ethics, society and its problems, literature, myth, history, sexuality, and so forth; and he has also authored novels and plays. He writes regularly for newspapers and magazines in Spain and abroad. In 1982, his book *La tarea del héroe (The Hero's Task)* won the National Prize of Literature.

THE FUTURE OF ETHICS

"Don Quijote let his will speak for him, and, in saying "I know who I am," he really meant "I know who I want to be." And it is man's desire to know what he wants to be, which is the underpinning of all human life. What you are is of little import to you; what is most essential is what you want to be." (Miguel de Unamuno, *Life of Don Quijote and Sancho*).

To speak of a "future" in relation to ethics entails several difficulties. In the first place, because of the very condition of ethics, which has nothing to do with the marvels or misfortunes that await us in the future but with the current custom of freedom, which has the greatest immediate priority. Morals, as the life it serves and to which it gives meaning, can never be left *for later*. Politics, for example, is an inversion of a more or less long duration, which supersedes present activity to determine future benefits. The legitimization of sacrifices necessary today or the current utilization of violence stems from our vision of the tomorrow which we are striving to attain. Ethics deals with opportune intervention at a critical moment *(kairós)*, with the choice that measures and causes us to keep or discard proposals of the present, not to achieve over the future but to give meaning to today; what counts is not what will obtain later but what is wanted now. The free individual does not seek in moral exercise anything distinct from himself or distinct from what is his due, but desires to go on deserving the confidence and the rational self-respect which he professes for himself. No future institution will exempt him from continuing to experience the undeniable urgency of the present option.

On the other hand, to refer to the "future" of ethics seems to take for granted that new fundamental values are brought together and that it is fitting to await (either with fear or with hope) a new type of morality. In a sense, this expectation is a foregone conclusion, if we refer only to the mores or customs. Erotic habits, political ideologies, family relationships, creative or destructive possibilities of applied science, when they are subjected to accelerated modification, will give way to codes of conduct different from those observed by our parents, and much more so from those of our grandparents. What was scandalous yesterday is today a fashion enjoyed without regard to scruples; behavior which yesterday was considered normal and edifying seems improper and brutal today. In this sense, a study of the future of ethics could be something like a futurological prognostication to determine which customs will be valued more highly in the future and which will decline slowly in the public esteem.

But this exposition does not take into account that the very root of the ethical perspective does not change as such the agitated rhythm of the modified custom. The code changes more or less but not the foundation that supports it. The sense and the justificatory root of the ethical attitude remain probably beyond modifications that are quite spectacular in their precepts. As a result, it is a lamentably hollow assertion to declare that a new moral paradigm takes firm hold every time that there is a change in the social attitude toward extramarital relations or in the death penalty.

But the most radical difficulty that presents itself for those who wish to investigate the future of ethics rests on assuring themselves that there will be ethics in the future. Don't we hear frequently that ethics is a simple superstructure inherited from the past which is about to be ousted by socioeconomics, psychoanalysis, biology or statecraft? The language of ethics now seems to be nothing more than a rhetorical concession destined to persuade the most gullible and misguided people or, more often, to discredit rivals in any power struggle. Those in possession of the greatest ethical fervor are recruited among the beautiful souls who love religion and attend Sunday sermons. As for the lay scientists of ethics, they commonly belong to the field of communications: they are cut in the mould of telephone operators but they pass themselves off as "holier than thou." What is more current is the reliance on moral language and sermons as a "light" substitute for antiquated political ideologies which are now in overt crisis. Moreover, the boldest ones say that we are living in a cynical age. Like the "western" in the movies, ethics seems destined to be only a future of "remakes," increasingly more artificial and more flattering, of the disease of nostalgia, until it comes about that there is no current practical reason for its existence and it ends up becoming a curious historical product, as a fossil in a museum.

To take the bull by the horns, as we Spaniards are wont to say, perhaps the issue of present-day cynicism is the most worthwhile beginning. In affirming the preponderance of cynicism or even its appropriateness, it seems that one subversively breaks with a series of traditional virtuous legitimizations, spoiled by the very sweet impotence of beautiful souls. But in reality, this provocation may be based on a misunderstanding. Cynicism is commonly only the attempted sincerity of the ingenuous. And sincerity is not within the scope of the ingenuous because the true act of being sincere can be attained by the one who previously has made the effort to know himself somewhat more than superficially, a task which promptly bores the ingenuous person. (The more ingenuous a person is, the more perversely malicious he believes himself to be.) In reality, the cynic is not the destructive scourge of the beautiful souls but his natural complement and, in most cases, his biographical destiny. The cynic is the beautiful soul several years later. He has not learned anything new, but what he always knew he interprets now upside down. Grounded in a moral outlook, since he does not beat around the bush, the beautiful soul always has believed that every virtuous act, to be authentic, must be an act of detachment, i.e., disinterestedness.

Later, he comes to the conclusion that the only detachment of which man is spontaneously capable has to do with the detachment of the retina and he concludes that virtue is a farce which should be abandoned. Regarding the ethical evaluation of what is political, the beautiful soul always supposed that the fitting commitment with the group implied the search for a commonly held good. When he then becomes convinced that the so-called common good is only institutional hostilily for the good of each one, he decides that open villainy is the least inconsequential political exercise. The beautiful souls always have believed that egoism is bad and altruism good. When informed later that one cannot help but be an egoist, he devotes himself to being one with the enthusiastic clumsiness of a neophyte, but he only manages to invert his old altruistic faith. And so the cynic does not become an egotist and remains instead a thwarted altruist.

The ethic of beautiful soul has, as a matter of fact, little future. Morality is disinterestedness, the fulfillment of duty out of pure respect for moral law, the renunciation of one's own self- interest for the benefit of another's interest or just for the sake of plain and simple disinterestedness. . . If the politically impeccable passes for the abomination of property and consumption, while at the same time demanding the destruction of any hierarchy that does not emanate directly and unequivocally from the suffering people and does not automatically uplift as a matter of course every person of humble station, then one must admit that ethics is suffering a crisis which could very well become irreversible. With its religious guarantee undermined and its civil foundation disenchanted or conflictive, the virtue of the beautiful soul has been converted into a hidden and incomprehensible quality, something like the "dormitive virtue" of Molière's doctor. But the certain thing is that the opium really has a definite effect on the human organism, although to resort to the dormitive virtue does not precisely help to understand it. In the same manner, virtue exists and functions, as the ethical perspective is implied in our most significant actions, although its purest justifications already turn out to be hardly believable. To approach the issue of the future of ethics, I will follow a path that is going to distance us a bit from the traditional moralizing as regards the dormitive virtue. We will set forth three themes: a) self-love as the foundation of ethics, b) virtue as individualism, and c) the active recognition of human rights.

a) Self-Love *(amour propre)* as a Foundation of Ethics.

The first thing that must be laid down is that the set of values, motives, precepts, pride and remorse which constitutes the scope of what is moral is not founded on any superhuman (divine) authority and not even on impersonal drives (genetic, preconscious, etc.), but on the conscious and creative dimension of human personality. This conscious and creative dimension of personality, simultaneously observes, craves, classifies, and has ambitions. In short, it *studies*, in the dual sense of learning and craving, what we are going to call human will. Morality comes directly and solely from the will: it is a desiring and a rejecting but never a disinterest. And it is pointless to say that it is a disinterested interest or a disinterest free of pathological connotation as Kant argues. Since the will is previous to the distinction among body, soul and spirit, the will becomes interested rationally, psychically and carnally in what concerns it. Only the will can rouse itself into action. It only focusses on itself; it never renounces anything except to grow better and only loves itself. And it never forgets its being (neither its own or the *Seyn*), because its wanting is the sharpest taking into account of what there is in fact, and the fact that this exists. This love for itself on the part of the will, this desire to conserve itself and persevere, to fulfill its potential, to experience the gamut of possibilities in search of the highest ones, to want to be transmitted and to perpetuate itself, is what must be understood by self-love.

What is moral is not the obligation of restricting self-love, but the consequent act of practicing its free play. This denomination of "self-love" is preferable to other equivalent ones, as for example "rational egoism" or "enlightened egoism," because, in reality, we are referring to something previous and subjacent to the psycho-social institution of the "ego": the I springs from the creative energy of self-love and not the opposite of this. To put it in a way that is necessarily enigmatic, self-love is "self" before being "mine." Furthermore, the invectives of Rousseau against *amour propre* for the benefit of *amour de soi*--the first would be vitiated by vanity and the competitiveness of society while the second would come directly from the exigencies of nature--reinforce in us the opposite meaning of this term (i.e., self-love). Human self-love can only be social, and by the same token can not be corporeal or reflexive. The most ethical dimension of self-love is precisely the recognition of what is human as such, the recognition of man *in* man, a basic requirement of community *philía*. Indeed, in self-love there is an eagerness not to lower one's esteem in the eyes of others. This essential search for conformity must not be confused with mere conformance since those "others" do not have to be in each specific historical moment the single historical majority, but those past, present or future ones in whom we recognize the exacting similarity of moral lineage. The search for excellence and the fear of being reproached by the best are not vain concessions to gregariousness but part of the mature acceptance of our *sociogenesis*, outside of which we would lose not only our present feeling of belonging but also the entire genealogy of identity and meaning. Finally, the term "love," in its traditional Platonic analysis as a dialectical combination of abundance and scarcity, as well as owing to its connotations of affective intensity, is perfectly adaptable to characterizing the tensional and projective character of the voluntaristic root of ethics.

The profound meaning of human self love--that is to say what we as human beings love and what we love when we are loving ourselves--is immortality. It does not involve the simple and rabid negation of death but the stubborn affirmation of life vis-à-vis the unavoidable certainty of perishing. It does not consist exclusively of the religious promise of an unending life after death, although this incredible promise and its ritual pomp doubtlessly spring from immortalizing self-love. Every culture is forged against death and the first function of each society is to make itself invulnerable instead of allowing the opening of wounds, to plot a certain immortality for its members. This not only consists of assuring survival but also of counteracting death, establishing memory where death causes oblivion, making something meaningful where death imposes absurdity, imposing order instead of chaos, ushering in pleasure instead of restoring insensitivity, setting up a hierarchy in place of definitive equality, establishing entertainment and diversion in lieu of boredom, making secure and not placing in jeopardy, making beautiful instead of exhibiting corruption, bringing novelty instead of never-ending routine, establishing abundance instead of despoiling, and assuring lineage so that there is a continuum of generations. It can be said that society and culture are always reactionary because there is nothing in them which does not suppose a reaction against the terrorist subversion of death. Thus death is not rejected but affirmed as a polemical task of life. Death is the contrast and verification of human life because it is not in the culture but in the totality of institutions and symbols that resist death as was preached some time ago of biological life. The essential and most significant nucleus of this resistance is to place freedom where death dictates necessity. This is precisely the task of ethics when self-love is put into practice.

Morality is, therefore, the most energetic consequence of finitude. Since its beginnings, it has consisted of performing the most intimate fiber of resistance and opposition to death. It has strength and glory where weakness and fear grow, compassion in face of those of us who do not have it, mutual support instead of unavoidable disintegration, transcendence versus perpetual banality, communication instead of sterile silence. . . Self-love is not only the will not to die but also of being immortal, that is to say, of establishing oneself and proceeding, despite death, so that it turns out to be subjugated by the vital human vocation. Outside of this spirited purpose which may be as ancient as man himself, there is only superfluous superstition in the ethical calling. One will probably say then that men have to be zealously moral since no one wants to die nor favor death. Where is the meritorious effort of virtue? What is certain, nevertheless, is that the discouraging tendency to surrender to death is a propensity as deeply rooted as the moral impulse itself. Pliny the Elder left us the saying that *nullum frequentius votum*--(there is) "no more common desire"--among men than that of dying. The very spasmodic impetus of self-love, if it does not manage to sustain itself by example, practice and reflection, becomes exhausted and turns out to be the ally of death. Together with the spirited personalizing voice of vital love for oneself there is never in absentia the depersonalizing whisper of narcotic annihilation. Why? What else is there? And afterward? Therefore one speaks without impropriety of moral "obligation" and "duty" because life is also obligation and duty, a resistance to inertia which sabotages our deepest sense of wanting. And since one cannot stop wanting, he who does not tire of wanting wants to become one with nothingness as Nietzsche warned.

The immoral temptation always consists of accepting a large part of the necessity of dying, so as to shield some watered down and spineless portion of immortality. Thus the general vigor which virtue seeks is lost and it becomes a fatal concession to that which one tries to avoid. Because the death of our moral sanity--not of course, the voluntary cessation of biological life which can be the highest confirmation of immortalizing self-love, that is, of the meaning of life--is never sought as an entity in itself but rather comes in opposition to itself, as a dissolution of a conflict which is not well understood or which we lack the courage to continue to countenance. It follows that it is to those who surrender their self-love to whom we could most appropriately pose the sad question which Rilke addressed to the nineteen-year old count of Kalkreuth who did away with himself:

> Did that alleviate you as you believed,
> or perhaps the cessation of living
> was still far from being dead?

b) Virtue as Individualism

Nothing is so frequently heard today as the individualism which is in force, whether it is to accept it as a difficult and recent conquest or to deplore it as a threat of a disintegrating lack of solidarity. Generally the way the notion of individualism is handled in both cases is skewed because of reduction and prejudice. There is no real opposition between individualism and society as there should be: individual autonomy is an invention of social evolution, as "sociable" as any other bond created by the collective imagination. The individual does appear not on the margin of society nor by any means against it, but as its most subtle and advanced product. As far as unity is concerned, its true enemies are those who suppose it to be not viable except for coercion or fusion. To the contrary, only the autonomous individual can really be responsible because only he can choose to be so or not. Tönnies spoke of the passing from community to society, from an organic unity to one that is mechanical. As far as I am concerned, I prefer to refer to passing from a logic of belonging to one of participation.

Individualism is the theoretical and practical recognition that the social center of operations and meaning, of legitimacy and decision, is the autonomous individual; that is, every single individual who makes up the social structure. There is not then a sense of community which transcends the sum or maximization of the interests of each one, nor is there a transcendent historical essence--nation, people or class--whose right to demand perpetuity and to impose sacrifices is above (that is, can renounce de facto or by law) the opportunity of fostering the welfare and freedom of all of its participants. In the field of ethics, which is what most interests us here, individualism supposes the moral enthronement of autonomy and responsibility of the individual above his belonging to a group or institution, to which he owes allegiance, and even above his belonging to a dissenting minority, a fact which is of no account with respect to the unanimity arrived at by consensus or imposed by other individuals. In the field of virtuousness, each individual is unique unto himself and not unto any institution, no matter how perfect and persuasive the institution, for in no instance can we dispense with the risk of opting for ourselves. Virtue can benefit many or the majority, but virtuousness is an attribute that can only be achieved on a personal level. The excellence of virtue, that which stimulates admiration for its dignity and glory, is the fact that at a particular moment *(kairós)* no one can be virtuous for another or be as exactly virtuous as another. In this sense, I have spoken at length on other occasions regarding the moral figure of the hero ("The Task of the Hero," "The Contents of Happiness"), who is very different from a bully. Rather, I tried to recapture the original sense of the term as Hanna Arendt explains it: "The origin of the word 'hero' is only the name given to each one of the free men who had taken part in the Trojan epic and to those about whom stories could be written. The idea of mettle, a quality which we consider indispensable for a hero to possess today, is found already in those who took it upon themselves to act and to speak, to insert themselves in the world and to begin their own story" (*The Human Condition*). *The hero is the autonomous individual who, in fulfilling or inventing the highest morality, decided to live his personal and social vicissitudes as an adventure that cannot be duplicated.* He does not seek originality at any cost, nor does he search for divergence or coincidence as far as the norm is concerned, but the establishment of his story as his own, as the fruit of his individualizing love.

He who asks at this advanced stage why it is better to be an autonomous individual than a slave or obedient child of the Great Mother does not deserve a reply. But it is evident that autonomy is a burden that is delicate and capable of causing guilt, subject to short circuits provided by our discouragement and also by the heteronomous nature of the prevailing political system. Short circuits which arise from the atavistic terror in having to personally place our signatures on our options instead of endorsing them to God or the Absolute Monarch, let alone the short circuits induced by bureaucratic economic and totalitarian alienation. It is onerous to have to agree reflexively and responsibly with the institution or the maintenance of community structures instead of simply accepting as a natural and predestined thing that we are a necessary part of them. In order to lighten this burden of the afflicted people or of the ignorant people who are maintained by the oligarchs, the contemporary state provides collectivizing mechanisms which permit and at times impose the abandonment of individual autonomy. In one of his posthumously published texts (*Omnes et singulatim*), Michel Foucault distinguishes pastoral power from state power. The latter regulates relations among citizens equal in rights and unequal in property, that is to say the public scene of metasubjective transaction. But pastoral power--a shameful supplement to state power that the state itself offers mixed in with the other power and often, by the intermediacy of propaganda, not discernible from the other power--reproduces the unlimited solicitude of the good shepherd for his sheep, entrusted with the task of ensuring that they are never alone nor disturbed. He is a benevolent dictator of their desires to prevent dangerous situations, a guide for their leisure time so that they do not succumb to vices or fall into the hands of unscrupulous merchants, and is ultimately responsible for the salvation of each one of them. This anti-individualistic and heteronomous pastoral power of the state (no less heteronomous even if its mode of legitimacy is very democratic), the promotor of a new common destiny, will solidly tie together all members through discussions supported by theocratic or medical arguments (for example, the case of the prohibition of drugs) or through simple functional rationalizations, and is not exclusive of totalitarian régimes. Many of those living under democratic régimes complain of the capricious isolation of individuals and of the risk they run in having so much solitude which may cause them to fall into networks of multinational traffickers. They are, without knowing it, demanding a "good" pastoral power of the state, that is, a privation of individual autonomy and responsibility which may turn out to be "safer" than the risks these deprivations may bring.

The system of individualistic political participation (inseparable in the last analysis from the individual ethical virtue) is conflictive, agonistic (in the sense of being cooperatively competitive) and scenic: it demands visibility and transparency. Does individualism tolerate a loss of will for civic participation? The diagnosis goes back to none other than Tocqueville ("in democratic societies, each citizen is habitually occupied in the contemplation of a very exquisite object which is himself") and is today repeated by numerous voices. Some like Benjamin Constant, and now Baudrillard, consider this lack of interest in the direct intervention in the public good like a peculiar, but not deplorable, characteristic of the "freedom of modern times," vis-à-vis the classic concept of citizenship. On the contrary, Hanna Arendt and also Agnes Heller, Castoriadis, etc., do not conceive of any authentic model of liberty without *vita activa* 'active life,' that is, without inexcusable participation in the management of the common good. I believe that it is important to emphasize that political participation (not the effusiveness in belonging to a group or party) is not the exclusive attribute of democratic dualism; hence its more differentiated and selective character, less automatic and, in a certain sense, more elitist. On the other hand, we may be witnessing the testing, although very inchoative, of forms of *vita activa* different from traditional ones but not less real. At any rate, that which is peculiar to individualism is not the withdrawal from politics and the retreat to privacy but the orientation of the intervention in the public welfare: its anti-collectivism. Collectivism is not characterized as being a form of production of wealth nor a distribution or ownership of such wealth, but the instrumental immolation of individual autonomy for the purposes of the collective entity which is something more significant and meritorious than the totality of its members.

"To engage in politics" in a collectivist sense is equivalent to subduing individuals through persuasion and discipline in order to achieve a "better" society based on the unity of its common destiny. The individualist can, and, in my opinion, must participate actively in politics and also with the purpose of bringing about a better society, but given that by this is understood a society which favors the appearance of individuals whose potential is more fulfilled, who are more autonomous and responsible, who are less guilty of being dependent on authority. The collectivist system works on individuals to condition them to the desirable society and the individualist system intervenes in the management of the social situation to facilitate the increase of possibilities and of the vitality of individuals.

c) The Active Recognition of Human Rights.

Undervalued several years ago by radical politicians who considered these human rights pious but hollow and bearing weakening effects on the revolutionary struggle, they were treated contemptuously and harassed by dictatorships which deemed them to be the Trojan horse, which was hypocritically paving the way for communist or capitalist penetration, whatever the case might be. Tossed about by the punctilious distrust of teachers of law and morals--for some they are too moral to be considered strictly "rights," for others they resemble positive rights too much in their legal claim of moral universality--human rights are today the most effective axiological contribution to the autoinstitution of a reasonably emancipated society. The ideological success of human rights has contributed to their being compromised. Originating in the affirmation of individual autonomy in opposition to statecraft, the polymorphism of the latter has enabled it to assimilate human rights to its own aims. Governments have the custom of brandishing them as a weapon to be hurled against neighboring states, while within their boundaries they consider them as comfortably and undeniably established since they no longer need to be watched. Some of those who champion human rights recall the appropriateness of Samuel Johnson's old dictum: "How is it that we hear the loudest yelps for liberty among the drivers of Negroes?" Human rights are transversal to politics, law and morality since they cannot be strictly contained in any of these fields nor erased from any one of the three. They do not constitute by themselves a system of politics, but they serve as a gauge to judge all and each one of them. They do not form part of a positive right, not even when they are collected together in the preamble of particular constitutions, but they keep the non-bureaucratically functionalist or repressive sense of each right. They reveal the moral project too normatively, but they contribute much more to give it flesh and blood than to distort it. If one can speak, as we attempt to do here, of a future for ethics, it must come through human rights.

What do they consist of? Of course, it does not have to do with promoting a new dialogue or modernizing an old one. Neither does the problem rest on giving a crystal-clear appraisal of any one of the most institutionally recommended lists since they wind up being incurable and necessarily circumstantial.

To allow some human rights means to be actively persuaded that the recognition of what is human is equivalent to the recognition of rights on the part of another individual who enjoys those same rights. It is not so much that man has one or another right but that he has the right to be a man, which takes into account the holding of rights, (or the individual as subject of the law), is a conscious and voluntary statute that men must morally concede to each other. The historical concretion of that right is articulated in a list directly related to the needs of man, which can be studied universally, and with his liberties which can be understood from the autonomy and responsibility of the individual participants in the community. Like every morally relevant idea, human rights start with a supposition that can never be completely reasoned out because it serves as a foundation for reasoning. In this case, that which approximates including all men as individuals is more worthy of esteem and perpetuation than what differentiates them as members of different political or cultural collectives. These differences are not considered irrelevant, but are only irrelevant insofar as they oppose respect for any of the essential coincidences. This question, which cannot be sufficiently emphasized, is not something obvious, irrefutable or in the realm of common sense . . . but a revolutionary conquest as well as an imposition. Therefore, do not ask all and each one of the servants of the *ancien régime* if they give their consent to change the formulation in which the question is couched, for as it were, the question remains valid. Rémy de Gourmont said that "civilization is only a series of insurrections" and the demand for human rights is the last and perhaps not the least important of the rebellions. It is an insurrection against theocracy, the extraordinary and transcendent establishment of community, the hierarchy of nature or of lineage, collectivist prejudices, statecraft, folkloric diversities that perpetuate the sacrifice of particularity for whatever universal aspects it has, and so forth.

The most resolute adversaries of the doctrine of human rights come ideologically from the left and the right. Some declare that human rights are an idealistic masquerade proclaimed by the bourgeois state to legitimize its dominion. Those who think that this is so are only somewhat retarded lowly officials--and not only in the temporal sense of the term--of the most harmful ideology of this century: Leninism. Under the pretext that every state is a deceitful dictatorship, they aspire--or have aspired in their day--to the unmasked imposition of the dictatorial state. The rights that the subjects--it is not fitting here to speak of citizens--claim from the governing power either take the form of resistance against it, which only represents the atomizing egoism of the petty bourgeois, or they coincide precisely with what the governing power prescribes no longer as a right but as an obligation for each party. In both cases, the claim winds up being proscribed. The passage of time has shown with sufficient clarity the success that the effective fultillment of Leninism could attain, which has curtailed the persuasive force of its argumentation.

But the most compact outcry against these rights arises from a different angle: from the so-called *nouvelle droite*--the parafascist right as it is known in the Spanish language--, and Third World anti-imperialism, no less reactionary but with a clear-cut leftist complexion. Accordingly, the pretentious universality of human rights supposes a Eurocentric violation of the cultural equilibrium of other groups dissimilar from the European tradition. The rights of each man do not hinge on an individual's belonging to the abstract universality regarding the human species but arises from their adherence to a specific people--from the traditions and way of interpreting the world peculiar to them--, which determine in the man a given identity and destiny. Individual human rights can undermine the cohesion of different people. Moreover, with the pretext of introducing human rights in other latitudes, what is meant to be imposed is the homogeneity of multinational exploitation: in a word, the new imperialism. Hence the most prudent among us claim--and this finds an echo in high international instances--the right of people to have self-determination, as something complementary of or even prior to the human rights of individuals. Third world tyrannies of different leanings receive generous economic support from more developed countries in the name of not interfering in the internal affairs of countries whose political peculiarities are as respectable as the criminal extravaganzas of Caligula. From an ethical-political point of view, it seems to me that the answer to these assertions must be of a clarity devoid of complex and belated repentance which today renew the evils of the worst colonialism of the past. It has not been wholly demonstrated that the institutional respect for human rights must be required to favor more the commerce of multinationals, but on the other hand, it has been proved over and over that those who seek folkloric license to trample them only claim to impose an autocracy which will be more difficult for its victims to tolerate than the omnipresence of McDonalds. And the ones who claim those rights are always the individuals in whose circumstances are brought together universal traits and the unrepeatable eventuality, and not the people or any other collective national identity.

Do we thus condemn the world to the monotony of the homogeneous, to proscribing customs and traditions which do not respect what the enlightened bourgeois individualism considers "human"? Well, such civilized monotony is unfortunately still too far away, even in countries that are supposedly more democratic. Before complaining of boredom, let us wait for boredom to set in. Would that the day arrive in which a certain ecology of human atrocity counsel that the following kinds of people be locked away in asylums: torturers, religious or nationalist fanatics, proponents of corporal punishment, racists, unruly people who practice flagellation of themselves or of others, etc.! At the present time, such examples of "diversity" are so common that we have much to do in attempting to extirpate them. The survival of wolves is not a question aesthetically and culturally raised until the time they stopped menacing the survival of human flocks. But what right do we "Westerners" have to impose our demand on the rest of the people in the world? The right of rebellion! Let us not forget that the democratic accomplishment is a revolutionary movement, that it neither can nor ought to be taken as anything else. Moreover, history demonstrates that in all parts of the world, no matter how "exotic," there are individuals who are "Western" by vocation, and accordingly they do not want to be so "different" as the nation to which they owe their cultural identity is fastidiously attached to its culture. Let us help them. The right to be different is undoubtedly respectable, but it must be taken into account that differences must be safeguarded, and that a right which protects all differences demands respect.

Human rights are perhaps locked in the filigreed outline of the common regulation--"Constitution," if you will--of the universal organization that sooner or later will reduce to a civilized sovereignty what is today unrestrained brigandage of nations. Then will there be accomplished one of the dimensions of the reasoned dreams of freedom which alerted people against the constituted states and their bellicose manipulation which enjoyed exemption from accountability. The humanity of five billion beings, their endemic and unjustifiable hunger, the nuclear threat, ecological catastrophes, all require this unitary code before it is too late. To this measure of political control will correspond what Hans Jonas (in *Das Princip Verantwortung*) says of "the ethics of broadened responsibility" which takes into account "the technologically accumulative collective behavior." One must disagree with the admirable Hannah Arendt regarding her statement that "a universal society can not mean more than a threat to liberty (*Interest in Politics*) since although the danger of supercontrol exists (science fiction has magnified it abundantly in its plots), the prevailing abuses, due to the absence of a supernatural authority, turn out to be more injurious than what was promised by a true universalist setting forth of this matter. The only serious objection to this arises from the difficulties that involve its being put into practice, and not from its hypothetical enslaving threats. At the present time, the ideological differences among the great blocs seem very attenuated by a general pragmatism that still retains ruthless streaks, but that is doubtless preferable to radical confrontation without compromise. On the other hand, there has sprouted a less rationalized and more visceral hostility, a new radical intransigency of a racial or theological nature more dangerous than the calculable conflict of interests, since it no longer is a matter of gaining something tangible but above all of exterminating the adversary. It is to be feared that although the abused egoistic interests are coming nearer little by little--always in conflict, however--, in men there sprouts the bloody conflict caused by the most atavistic types of incompatibility, a ferocious trace, perhaps definitively ineradicable, of what ancient wisdom called our original sin.

Ethics of a willful taking of a stand, the reflexive and stylized fruit of human self-love, a wager for the vitalistic immortality of men, milenarian members of a community enterprise of self-perpetuation whose most elaborate fruit is the autonomous and responsible individual capable of acknowledging and working with his equals. Everything in ethics is immanence and humanism, except for superstition, which is only concealment by heteronomy or betrayal of immanence and humanism. Ethics' problem for today and for tomorrow, once its refuge in transcendence is abandoned, is how to avoid falling into intranscendence, that is, into banality. With respect to Nazi horrors, Hannah Arendt spoke of the banality of evil and we could still refer to banality as evil, that is to say the destructive undertow of the abandonment of transcendence. Despite what some moralists suppose, the current ethical difficulty is not cynicism, but banality, that which is instrumentally and capriciously intranscendental. What is essential in this is the performance of the creative imagination of new ideas, forms and values (whose undertaking Nietzsche set forth with unequalled provocative clarity and later was discussed by Castoriadis and

Victoria Campa in Spain) because ethics is a *wanting to be*, and since Aristotle's *De anima* we know that "no being desires without imagination." Although the basic frame of values has already been established and in it there are concurrent agreements which we have not chosen to or are able to reject, the forms in which the moral style of each person in each epoch will be depicted, do not permit the closing of the litany or of the respectful formalism of the law. Nothing remains then regarding the ethics of the future which enlivens our present, except to use once more the still pertinent dictum of Ortega: "Therefore, every morality will be immoral if among its duties there does not prevail the primary one of finding ourselves constantly prepared to make reforms, corrections and increase the ethical ideal. Every system of ethics which orders the perpetual imprisonment of our free will within a closed system of evaluation is ipso facto perverse" (*Meditations on the Quijote*).

[Translation on an essay requested by the editor]

EDUARDO SUBIRATS

Eduardo Subirats was born in Barcelona in 1947. He was educated in a German school in Barcelona. In 1972 he began to study philosophy in Spain and later he continued these studies in France and Berlin. After several years spent abroad, he returned to Barcelona in 1979 where he taught aesthetics at the School of Architecture while working on his doctorate which he received in 1981. From 1981 to 1983 he lived in New York City where he taught classes and did research on architecture. He returned to Madrid and later taught and wrote in Mexico, Brazil and Argentina. In recent years he generally has lived part of the year in Toledo, Spain and the other part in Berlin. He was a visiting professor at Princeton University in 1990 and 1991. Of the more than ten books he has written, he considers *La cultura como espectáculo (Culture as Spectacle)* [1988] and *El alma y la muerte (The Soul and Death)* [1983] to be the most important. The first-mentioned work is synthesized in the essay included in this book and the second deals with the relationship between the rational tradition and mysticism.

SCREENED EXISTENCE

The philosophical ideal of a culture fashioned like a work of art, in which human existence could recognize the complete fulfillment of its potentialities and aspirations, its creativity and liberty, has been carried out. The artistic shape or design of what is real has been universally elevated to a reality principle in late industrial society. The utopias of an organization of work which would bring together the characteristics of artistic creation have been accomplished. In the universe of the media of mass communication, as in the production of consumer products or urban planning, art is the positive principle of the make-up of reality.

But the perfectly fashioned reality has not exiled the alienation of existence, the external forms of control and conditioning of the individual, nor the social emptiness and despair. The production of an aesthetically programmed universe does not eliminate nor surpass the physical and aesthetic degradation of natural or metropolitan environments, the threat to survival that weighs on modern conscience, the aggressive and destructive sense of scientific-technical progress or the anguish of history. The world of the spectacle stands rather as a substitutive reality, a kingdom of a technically synthesized transcendence.

In the cultural theories formulated in the context of aesthetic and ethical values of the Renaissance, as well as in Vico, Herder or Hegel, the classical ideal of a universal and harmonious order prevailed under the definition or the utopia of an artistic condition of culture. The most beautiful expression of this perspective is due to Giambattista Vico. For him, poetry, music, song and dance were to be considered as the original principle, the constitutive factor of culture, both in what pertains to their artistic manifestations and in what relates to their human needs and useful activities, and, ultimately, to knowledge.

We associate the dissolution of this artistic ideal with the advent of industrial society and the prevalence of monetary values of rationality, technological functionalism and the bureaucratic formalization of modern society. This was, in fact, the story of the art criticism which such intellectuals and artists as Ruskin and Morris stirred up in the 19th century as a protest against a socially and aesthetically degraded order not in harmony with human existence. This was also true of the cultural panorama reflected by the pioneers of scientific sociology, mainly in the case of Weber, and, more specifically, in the analyses of Tönnies and Simmel on the decline of European historical culture, that is, of that cultural formation based on ethical and aesthetic values.

The concept of industrial culture, critically developed from the perspective of constituent value, at the same time that it proves itself reductive of rationality in the totality of human manifestations and that it highlights the subsidiary questions of alienation that the reproductive process of society imposes on all spheres of life (Marx), on the analysis of the instinctive renunciations required of the individual (Freud) and on the theses of dishumanization of modern society (Ortega), pointed, directly or indirectly, to this same nexus of the dissolution of the cultural ideals espoused by the enlightened and classicistic bourgeoisie of the 19th century. The machine era could have definitively ended the beautiful dreams of an artistic culture.

These negative visions of modern culture, including the very critical theory of Adorno and Horkheimer, did not include an aspect which I consider decisive in the so-called advanced societies of today and which I want to call "the production of the spectacle" (see my book *Culture as Spectacle [La cultura como espectáculo]*, Madrid, 1988). Two historical facts seem significant in this discussion, the programs of the artistic vanguards of the beginning of the century, in which a new social model conceived as a technical artistic simulacrum was set out, and the political national-socialist utopia as a work of art. Le Corbusier may be remembered as the most brilliant exponent of this transformation of art and architecture in the media, technologically and rationally defined, in its global design of life, starting from the experiential conditions of a minimalized individual existence and ending with the urban macro-projects which include the programming of the new industrial civilization as a whole. On the other hand, German national socialism forged the utopia of a revolutionary conception of power not under strictly institutional dimensions, not even under ethical-heroic or theological-political dimensions, but precisely as a total configuration of human life and society in the manner of a great work of authentic art.

The conception of architecture and art in general as a medium of the portrayal of human existence on the stage and the idea of politics as the production of mass spectacles, as Le Corbusier and Goebbels formulated it, rely on a firm theoretical tradition. But its importance in today's developed societies is due rather to the coincidence of a new faith in images and the enormous degree of development of technical means capable of satisfying this iconic demand of society.

Among the new aspects of contemporary industrial society, the value of image as giving form to social activity stands out. It is a well-founded commonplace that the face of a president, or what one may call its aesthetic characteristics, constitutes, by itself, and actually supplants in many instances the function that ideological contents, propagandistic slogans and political programs formerly performed. In this sense, "the new era of incredulity has fortified a surrender to images," writes Susan Sonntag. The motto of "politics as a work of art" is contained in the design of an image (of a president, an institution or an historical event) as an instrument for shaping of the public life from its urban or natural place of origin to its reproduction in the media of reality through the technical systems of communication. "Politics as a work of art" has been accomplished in the form of the production of the existence of each individual as a montage of the media.

It is as if everything, the interior and urban space in which vital events occur, the great decisions which affect the future of humanity, the objectives which dominate the daily life of each statistically defined individual, and the values, symbols and expectations which govern the social future in its entirety, were the result of a design, a programming or an external conformation, like a great cosmological or sacramental spectacle, now raised to an industrial configuration. As indeed they are: The great world of the small screen, or the life system which globally defines the plan of new cities, offer models of the total administration of life starting from an artistic-technological principle, that is to say, in the image of an art work made on the scale of modern industrial technology. The modern definition of institutional and political power coincides with the programming of culture as spectacle.

This notion of spectacle and the resulting critical theory of modern culture which is put forth demands the modification of many of the conceptions and presuppositions about society, power, culture or democracy which we have traditionally assumed, and give high priority to the revision of the concept of human existence as its own agent or protagonist. Values like those of work and leisure, the habits and norms of human life, our desires and expectations, the opinions we form about the world and its things, in short, what we call life, present a new perspective when one keeps in mind the double conditioning to which individual existence is subject. This existence is a variable in a total scenario (that of urban or interior spaces, systems of communication, bureaucratic organization of socialization, and knowledge), and that of being the passive spectator of a previously organized and produced reality. Such is the psychotic condition of the modern soul.

Human life has been reduced to the terms of a "screened existence." Screens put us in contact with the world, screens give an account of our aspirations and desires, screens form and inform, screens keep watch, record, produce, create, screens give our account of our gestures and our body, and of our illness as well as of our happiness. But what is real is converted into spectacle just as individual existence acquires through this the illusory quality of a scenic effect. The individual is formed during the course of an indefinite process of reproduction of norms, clichés, arrangements and conditioning and through them, the concepts of existence, of subjectivity and of action are revealed objectively as statistically quantifiable variables.

The virtual or chimerical characteristic of existence as a dream is an old literary motif of the short religious plays of the Spanish baroque period. In these plays human life was identified precisely with the staging, with the "great theater of the world," just as the spectator of today adheres to the spectacle of the small screen as his deepest and most authentic reality. But with the devaluation of earthly existence, and with the production of a second reality ontologically more intense than real, the modern spectacle adds a substitutive dimension which was absent from the conception of classical theater. In that second reality, the technical production of the imaginary is called upon to supplant what is real, meaning its life and its conflicts, its character regarding the unknown and the unconscious as well as regarding survival and creation. In the fulfillment of culture as spectacle, art has died as the experience of what is real and as mimesis and mystery, by the same token, its absolute fulfillment is postulated as a universal design of an existence that translates into the stage effect the screen gives forth. Nevertheless, our screened existence appears at the same time as the redemption of the individual's real being, stigmatized today as in the most obscurantist ages of Christianity, with the negative signs of the vain or the chaotic, the conflictive or ephemeral, in the divine machinery of the new industrially produced spectacle of the world.

Paul Scheerbart, one of the pioneers in the aesthetics of the modern skyscraper, conceived, together with Bruno Taut, a city of the future, luminous, immaterial and geometric, whose reverberations, transparencies and crystalline formations were meant to announce a new transcendent and apocalyptic era. The metaphors of ideal cities constructed as crystalline crowns, radiant mountains and luminous structures are found as a matter of fact among the vanguard utopias of the twenties. They even persisted in the nocturnal architecture of national socialism: characterized by the fulfillment of an absolute order of the imaginary or metaphysical city, which transcends, with spectacular signs of fascination and enthusiasm, the real destruction of the classical-modern city of the nineteenth century. The apocalyptic myth of the modern metropolis and the corresponding psychic disposition it gives rise to in the beholder, leads at the same time to a fascination with finality, emptiness and destruction, which in fact poses a threat to the very existence of the individual, and which has not stopped being repeated in the great artistic emblems of the twentieth century. The syndrome *Metropolis, King Kong* and *Blade Runner* constitutes one of multiple examples.

In the same sense that Scheerbart or Taut announced poetically the redemption of the city in the reverberated order of fictititous heavenly cities, the modern production of culture as spectacle is stylized as the beginning of social salvation.

We often ask ourselves if the course of wars around the globe will end one day, if the destruction of the biosphere will stop or if the limitless growth and limitless social, economic or aesthetic deterioration of the industrial megalopolises will lead to an ultimate collapse. Such issues should not be considered! Critical philosophy of the first half of the century saw in the growing negative phenomena of industrial civilization the sign of a limit both historical and spiritual. There were predictions about the end of the Enlightenment, the death of art, the end of man, a post-historical age, and the death of philosophy. The edifying alternatives facing so many allegories of a final era were not and are not more encouraging. They brought the age of mechanization, wholly computerized social order, an atomic State, techno-culture, and so forth. One might say that modern man has assumed very much his negative historical condition as in the apocalyptic conceptions of medieval Christianity. It no longer seems even thinkable to us to have a constituent spiritual sense of history and of human existence.

But nothing of all that announces either an apocalypse or the end of time, although it probably augurs the coming of a new age. A culture collapses. Its decline has already been announced more than a century ago. Another one is born.

At that juncture, the category of spectacle as a sign of our next becoming comes into being. The future no longer belongs to the order of a tehnological domination. Millenarian utopias based on the demiurgic power of technology also constitute a romantic dream. No one can believe any longer in the socially and historically marshalling power of techno-science in this era of ecological disasters. While art, in that programmatic, integrating and shaping sense of human reality which distinguished the aesthetic revolution of historical vanguards, that is the art that was conceived in close interdependence with technological and political power--in the sense in which a Le Corbusier or a Goebbels wielded it--can produce a new experience of what is real, a new human prototype, new identifiying symbols, integrative values, in short, the new culture, and it is creating them effectively.

The urban utopia of expressionism which superimposed an imaginary city and culture on the real city and culture, both of which were threatened by social crises and the degradation of cultural forms, has, in the meantime, taken on an universality of existence in those aspects which have to do with the twofold process involving the coming together of art and technology. On the one hand, art has lost its social function as an individual form of reflective communication, to the benefit of technical and bureaucratic systems of the reproduction of what is real; on the other hand, the new technologies have progressively adopted formal and formative tasks which formerly were the specific task of the cultural or social role of art. Just as the crisis of the communicative and reflective function of art and its closeness to technical forms of production and reproduction originated the aesthetic revolution of vanguards, so the combination of a new "extended" concept of art organically linked with the technologies of communication and information, has generated a new conception and understanding of culture. Techno-imaginary production, techno-artistic creation of "responsive environments," "screened existence" or production of the spectacle are several other concepts that focus in on the analysis of this new cultural situation.

This perspective on contemprary culture suggests something more than the critique of an alienating reason relating to civilization. It also supposes a third term in the division between an artistic, ethical or humanistic culture and technological culture, since the technical production of the cultural spectacle includes both at the same time. But, above all, this synthesis of the total work of art with technological power (or to express it with another image, the fulfillment of history as a great Eucharistic play, using modern industrial resources) eliminates that inner tension or that dialectic between progress and destruction, or between human enlightment and regression. The panoramas of critical philosophy of the twentieth century have been based on this.

It is not exactly a matter of an artistic utopia of classicist or romantic idealism. We are rather facing an "aesthetic education" which has abdicated, nevertheless, its idealistic presupposition: the fulfillment or plenitude of the human individual, whose chimera has leaped through the air like all the other myths of modern Enlightenment. One must rather look for its new aesthetic premises in the doctrines of logical games, the theory of systems, computer science, behaviorist psychology, and statistics.

Under current epistemological dimensions, politics and aesthetics, the production of the cultural spectacle embraces a final conciliatory function or a renewed mission which is both redemptive and universal. Of course it no longer deals with great philosophical discourses on emancipation, history, the subjective consciousness of the individual or *Bildung*, or of their historical precedents, or even the Christian doctrine of a successful salvation in the after-life. Since it is more circumspect from a theological and philosophical point of view, in an epoch in which the great metaphysical values have lost their legitimate function and therefore their former rhetorical splendor, the culture of the spectacle does not in a lesser sense fulfill a high metaphysical and transcendent purpose. In their own realm (the audiovisual media or post-modern architecture constitute exemplary models), the conflicts of this world are overshadowed, and insubstantiality and life's woes surrender their earmark in exchange for the images of a vital and redeemed identity, a rediscovered happiness and an absolute being, even through it takes the less noble figure of the heroic virtues of a detergent, the historically universal significance of a president's smile, or the resurrection of a doric column that has become sacred again. The fully dominated world continues to be split and fragmented, but it continues to be precisely the old negative condition which makes of its spectacular representation the new human redemption in a transcendence by the media.

The analysis of culture as spectacle must be aware of its limits. The principles of technical effectiveness and economic efficacy to which technical systems of communication are subject, the radical abstraction and banalization of the linguistic contents which institutional and techno-economic conditions impose on these contents, their subordination to economic interests or to relationships of power disclose the unilateral and ideological character with which the realistic and universalist claim of the spectacle is burdened. But, above all, it is its tendency to deny, to repress reality as experience, to supplant reality as a techno-imaginary product, which today reveals the techno-artistic production of cultural spectacle as a regressive utopia or enterprise.

The spectacle is not real in the same measure as the object is in Kant's theory of knowledge, that is to say, as a synthesis of real data in the artificially constructed unity of experience. As a world of the screen, as a reduction of existence to its images, as a total environment or integrally programmed space of private and public life, the cultural spectacle plays the same ontological and symbolic role that nature does in the Age of Enlightment or the concept of the Supreme Being in Christian theology. The spectacle is real in an absolute sense because only as regards this condition does it enjoy an ontological fullness in itself, for from this state of being authentically and truly existent can there come to the surface a second reality, or can there occur a reinforced order of things. This is so despite the fact that the spectacle is a simulacrum of what is real, a second nature or an artificial universe. And in that naturalism or hyperrealism which the spectacle adopts, the model of which is constituted by audiovisual means of communication, resides its regressive moment, its resacralizing principle of culture.

In modern culture, in which neither images, nor words, nor instruments are sustained in a sacred conception of the world, nothing and nobody can really guarantee its principle of authenticity or truth, or its real character in an absolute sense. Notwithstanding, we know that the total interaction, the techno-genetic manipulation, the spectacular permutation of history, the simulated cabins, the recycling, the synergetic acceleration of information and the perception of automated war are, in effect, more real than our experience or our existence individually and collectively taken into account. Dematerialization, deconstruction of the real, abstraction and the negation of reality are some categories which, in modern art as in the culture of the media, precisely define this negative relationship of modern man with what is real within the framework of his individual experience. They define ultimately that psychotic condition which incapacitates today's average man in his attempt to confront directly and individually, life and death, love and destruction, in short, what is real according to that principle of rational autonomy, and the moral integrity of the person as defined by the modern ideal of self-awareness and morality. Techno-artistic culture tends to dislodge the real from human existence at the same time that it imposes itself as the most authentic reality, as what is real in an absolute sense, although it is impenetrable to the experience it denies through a universe of products, norms and conditionings. Between a publicity image and the massive consumption of a specific product, there does not exist a casual or logical relationship but a miraculous connection which only its statistical translation knows how to hide. Removed from individual experience, reality is then imposed on this experience under the form of a product. But this relationship presupposes the resacralization of the product, the object, or of the image which they embody and which allows them to be elevated to this miraculous dimension.

The transformation of the contemporary vanguard, the theatrical ritualization of the work of art as an expositive object, the resacralization of the artist as a "star," today constitutes the true path leading to the spectacular regression of culture. Its complement is the destruction of what is real under the imaginary universe of new technologies of the spectacle, together with the new technologies of an economic progress that have an objectively destructive sign. But that destruction constitutes also its radical limit.

To assume this experience of what is real in artistic reflection and to derive its critique from this reflection constitutes a necessary and renewed vision of enlightment for today.

[Translation of an essay requested by the editor.]

EUGENIO TRIAS

Eugenio Trías was born in Barcelona in 1942. He studied philosophy at the University of Barcelona where he received his master's degree in 1964. He received his doctorate in philosophy in 1980 with a dissertation on Hegel that was published as a book the following year. Trías later obtained the chair of Aesthetics and Composition at the Barcelona School of Architecture. Several of his books have won prizes, especially the highly acclaimed *Lo bello y lo siniestro (The Beautiful and the Sinister)*, which won the National Essay Prize in 1983. The second edition of this book came out in 1988, and it is from this edition that the material included in this collection has been taken.

THE BEAUTIFUL AND THE SINISTER

"The beautiful is the beginning of the terrible which we can still endure." (Rainer Maria Rilke)

"The sinister (*Das Unheimliche*) is that which should remain hidden but has been revealed." (Schelling)

This part of the book is devoted to reflecting on these two aphorisms. The hypothesis to be evolved is the following: the sinister constitutes a condition and boundary of the beautiful. As far as its condition is concerned, an aesthetic effect cannot be achieved at all without the presence of the sinister in an artistic work. With regard to boundary, the revelation of the sinister destroys *ipso facto* the aesthetic effect. Consequently, the sinister is a condition and a boundary. It must be present while apparently absent. It cannot be revealed. It is at the same time the cipher and source of power for the artistic work, a cipher of its magic, mystery and fascination, a source of its capacity for suggestion and rapture. But the revelation of that source implies the destruction of the aesthetic effect. The illusory character of art, at times conceived of as fraudulent, resides in this inducement of suspense, the vertigo that accompanies the aesthetic effect must be seen in this paradoxical connection. Insomuch as the beautiful borders on what must not be shown, art is acrobatic: the beautiful is "the beginning of the terrible which can be endured." Thus the sinister is "the revelation of that which must remain hidden," and immediately produces the rupture of the aesthetic effect.

Art today--movies, narration, painting--travels through a dangerous road: it tries to clarify that boundary and that condition which are revealed in such a way that makes for the preservation of aesthetic effect. Is such a thing possible or are we touching upon an impossibility? Set on this course, the cathartic nature of art can find its most eloquent expression. As Novalis wrote: "Chaos must shine in the poem under the unconditional veil of order."

To go beyond the limiting framework of aesthetics based on the beautiful was the sum total endeavor of Kantian philosophy, of the German idealism that prolonged it, and of romanticism. It will be necessary, first of all, to evoke succinctly that revolution which renders intelligible Rilke's poetry, without which an aesthetics limited to the traditional category of beauty would not be conceivable. Kant's analysis of the sublime means, in this sense, the Copernican revolution in aesthetics: the enjoyment of aesthetic pleasure beyond the formal principle, measured and confined to the restricted traditional concept of the beautiful within which its boundaries had been set. This adventure to the beyond (to the infinite) caused its limiting foundations to totter as it inclined toward abysses of sublimity and horror, in search of uncompromising unity, and paved the way for the transition which was to take flight with the blossoming of romanticism and which saw the blending of the sublme and the sinister. It will be necessary to dwell, first of all, on the Kantian analysis of the sublime and to enter subsequently into the analysis of the romantic treatment of the sinister. In this way we will fashion the pillars that sustain the hypothesis to be developed.

From the Beautiful to the Sublime

The presupposition prevails, since Classical Antiquity, that the beautiful implies harmony and a right proportion. While the Platonists and neo-Platonists, both in ancient times and during the Renaissance, essentially conceived of beauty in its pure spiritual and luminous simplicity, they did not fail to accept that limiting and formal character of harmony and proportion among the parts when defining lesser beauty in the world of sentient appearance. Aesthetics rooted in Stoicism and materialism as well as the aesthetics of beauty conceived as a luminous idea--aesthetics of harmony and light--coincided in defining the beauty of its sentient presentation in terms of measure and of limitation. Their unity, with respect to the aesthetics which began to flourish around the middle of the eighteenth century, lies in their coincidence in rejecting from the sphere of what is beautiful all that implies or suggests disproportion, disorder, infinitude and chaos. In fact, limitation and perfection was, for the Greeks, an unquestionable equation. Evil, ugliness, falseness and irrationality were synonyms of the limitless and of infinity. The imperfect and the infinite were the same. This proposition, questioned first by patristic theology (and since Nicholas of Cusa, in the Renaissance, by philosophy and the "New Science"), maintains its legitimacy in the sphere of aesthetics until the eighteenth century, demonstrating the truth of Hume's reflection concerning the establishment of and the unshakable force of aesthetic "beliefs" and habits. It is as if sensitivity maintained allegiances which the spirit had rejected, thus holding back the revulsive effects of the new systems of thought. Of course, the anti-Greek ideas of St. Basil and of St. Gregory of Nisa, which came close to those of St. Augustine regarding plenipotentiary and infinite divinity, are not a defined and limiting form or idea, but are in collusion with gnosis, a foundation without foundation, an abyss, an infinitude. They are ideas sensitized in images which opened for the first time the whole range of the sublime: the deep sea, the ever burning bonfire (which Moses had witnessed), the expanse of the ocean and the desert sand, and the blinding light, the very potent light which is darkness in every sense of the word. All these images, prepared in a form characterized by that swan song of Greco-Roman antiquity, were the postulates of neo-Platonism, which predisposed the spirit to accept in a wordly way the notion of infinity. Nevertheless, this acceptance is only brought to completion with difficulty and with authentic baptisms of blood, a completion which is at the core of the Renaissance spirit.

In this context, it is not possible to explain the historical mode through which, with a good measure of difficulty, the most contrary equation to the Greek spiritual core is imposed, the identity of which hinges on infinitude and perfection. It can be only pointed out that this idea, suggested by Judeo-Christian theology, opens up the field to a possible reflection on the *positive infinite* as an ontological and epistemological category which, around the middle of the eighteenth century, came to the fore in the aesthetic realm, thus subverting completely human sensivity and taste.

The category of the sublime, thoroughly explored by Kant in his *Critique of Judgment* means the definitive crossing of the Rubicon, the extension of aesthetics beyond the limiting and formal cetegory of the beautiful. As the feeling of the sublime can be awakened by natural sentient objects which are negatively conceived, lacking in form, shapeless, out of proportion, rootless, chaotic, such as a trip through the Alpine mountains can stir up, and such as a blinding vision of a storm or the perception of an indefinite extension of material mass are able to suggest desolation and slow death. In this way, an Arabian desert breaks the yoke, the *non plus ultra* of sentient thought inherited from the Greeks, opening routes toward the Mare Tenebrarum. Romanticism was responsible for the exploration of the new continent, initiated by Kant in a decisive and resolute way.

A Stagecoach Trip toward Impossible Landscapes

One afternoon at the beginning of the last century, a distinguished middle-aged lady was crossing by stagecoach an especially wooded and uninhabited zone of Great Britain. Through the curtain or the window could be seen a sky filled with menacing clouds. Facing her was a very old eccentric man, dressed as a poorly shaven beggar, who did not lose the chance to examine the slight changes in the light and atmosphere of the landscape. Suddenly what was feared occurred, a downpour, a cloudburst, thunder, lightning, at the same time that it was becoming dark and that the stagecoach shook up the passengers, who tried to adjust the windows and curtains so as to avoid being exposed to the strong gusts of wind and the torrents of rain. And then the old passenger, who shared the same compartment with the distinguished lady, opened the window and stuck out his head, neck, and half of his torso, remaining rigid and without motion in that difficult position, defying the movement of the vehicle and the inclement weather. In a barely disguised stupor, the woman could not understand what the half-mad old man was doing in that strange position. The old man stayed that way for about an hour until he abandoned his astonishing contemplation of the landscape, and utterly soaked, resumed his seat as he offered excuses for his extraordinary behavior. Finally, the timid woman decided to ask him what he was so eagerly looking for or simply what he was looking at. And the old man answered that he "had seen sights that were marvellous and never witnessed before." Piqued with curiosity, the woman opened the window half way, at first stuck out only her head and then more of her torso. The old man had suggested that she keep her eyes wide open. She repeated what the eccentric man had done and the sights she saw with her wide-open eyes were truly impossible.

Years later, the same lady, who usually resided in London and had friends who were art fanciers, decided to satisfy her own curiosity about an exposition of a controversial painter, an eccentric named Turner, who, in the opinion of his adversaries, painted what no human eye had seen (even his own, of course). While she wandered about the exposition and before observing the canvasses which seemed to have certain yellow and green spots, she entertained herself by listening to the comments of knowledgeable people who were sure that nowhere on the planet Earth did there exist images claimed as valid by that mad painter of the fantastic. The opinions were so negative and the pictures gave forth such signs of mockery and outright ridicule that the lady, moved perhaps by pity, decided finally to halt and contemplate one of the compositions, the one that was closest to her. And lo and behold, with ill-concealed surprise, she saw the very thing she had seen years before through the window of the stagecoach. Then she understood who that mad old beggar sitting opposite her in the stage coach was. And struck with the intent of restoring in her mind the credibility of that painter, she began to shout, in the midst of all those who were attending the exposition, "But I saw it, I saw all this with my own eyes!"

Is it necessary to recall that still in the middle of the eighteenth century, a traveler condemned to travel through the Alps for business reasons "lamented those chaotic forms devoid of grace and beauty, that compendium of horrors and ugliness that characterize the Alps with their repugnant snowy expanses, their malformed irregularity of glacial masses?" Of course, the traveler would close the window and the curtain in order not to see such frightening things.

These anecdotes are sufficient to demonstrate the change that takes place in the sensitive outer skin of Western man in the twilight of the eighteenth century. The Kantian reflection on the sense of the sublime must be taken as the most solid support of the new perception of nature and of the landscape which was a product of the enlightened century, a century secretly enamored of shadows.

The Kantian Analysis of the Sense of the Sublime

In the first place, the individual understands something grandiose (very much above him in material expanse) which produces in him the sensation of shapelessness, disorder and chaos. The immediate reaction to the spectacle is distressing: the individual feels that he is in a state of suspension in front of that object which transcends him and goes beyond him. He feels it as a menace which threatens his integrity. There follows a first reflection on his own insignificance and impotence in face of the object which is not measurable in magnitude. But that anguish and that vertigo, which are painful, are fought against and conquered by a second reflection, superimposed upon and blended with the first, in which the individual rises from the awareness of physical insignificance to a reflection on his own *moral* superiority. This is possible when the immeasurable object physically and appreciably stirs up an Idea of Reason in the individual. It is an idea which is by definition distinct from the concept of understanding, a conception of the infinite (in our soul, in nature, in God). The infinite physical object sensitizes the rational-moral idea of infinity. Thus the individual achieves awareness of his own *moral* superiority with regard to nature, which, nevertheless, evokes and stirs in him, despite its apparent chaotic, disorderly and desolate state, the Idea of infinity presented as being impressive and spectacular. The infinite thus infiltrates our amphibious nature of carnal spirits. It is a mental process whose path consists of five stages:

1. The perception of something grandiose which suggests the idea of the formless, indefinite, chaotic and limitless.

2. The suspension of the mind and consequently painful feeling of anguish and fear.

3. The awareness of our insignificance in face of that immeasurable magnitude.

4. The reaction to sadness through a feeling of pleasure derived from the understanding of the formless form by means of an idea of reason (the infinitude of nature, the soul and God).

5. A mediation fulfilled between spirit and nature by reason of the sensitization of infinity. Through the pleasurable feeling of the sublime the infinite becomes finite, the idea becomes flesh, the dualisms between reason and sensitivity, morality and instinct, and divinity and phenomenon are overcome in a unitary synthesis. Man "touches" that which surpasses and frightens him (the immeasurable); the divine becomes present and patent through the human being, in nature: wherewith, the destiny of man on earth, given this privileged situation, remains manifest. Romanticism will do no less than elevate to an agenda and an artistic exercise this ideological background advanced by the old Kant of the *Critique of Judgment*.

The sense of the sublime, in its full ambiguity and ambivalence, is found between pain and pleasure. The object which brings it into play should, theoretically, cause pain in the subject. It is an object which could spell destruction for the subject who comes in close contact with it and is able to grasp it. This object can be a hurricane, a cyclone, a typhoon, or something which at least constitutes for the subject a distressing threat, like the boundless ocean or the desolate desert. It was not without good reason that the desert was considered by old dualistic Manichean religions the dwelling place of the prince of hell, the very kingdom of Nothing or the sentient emergence of the unfounded and bottomless abyss. In order to be enjoyed--a Kantian requirement of the aesthetic sense--the object must be contemplated from a distance; only in this way could the "disinterested" character of contemplation be assured.

But the subject experiences at the same time a pleasurable feeling, the result of an internal conflict which is superimposed on the fear and anguish through a more powerful feeling of pleasure, which, tinged and filtered by that fear and that anguish, becomes sharper. And Kant sought the source from which the subject extracts that pleasure, and which acts as a counterweight to the menacing violence of the object.

This directs critical thought along the lines to which it characteristically adheres, by diverting attention from the object to the subject. The solution to this question is to be found in making explicit the structures of the subject. The material object is only a pretext and an opportunity for the subject to stir up some of its faculties. But, one must not forget that the pretext and opportunity as a sentient piece of data, is the indispensable condition for bringing about that stirring up. The question, then, is what are the faculties that have been stirred up?

Of course, it is not the intellect, in face of the sentient datum formalized by the structures of sensitivity, space and time, which adds a restrictive and fixed concept not suitable for the understanding of what exceeds form and limitation. The intellect, doomed to explore the island of reason and to shape the categorical map through which it determines sensorial contents, can know nothing of what is situated beyond the coastal beaches, leaving to reason the uneasy and distressing question of all that which exceeds those visual frontiers: that which surpasses its horizon. Consequently, the intellect serves no purpose with regard to an object which suspends every limit. At this juncture the sense of the sublime differs from that of the beautiful. Kant's thinking on the latter point presupposes the intervention of the intellect, devoid of concepts, on the sentient datum through the imagination by virtue of which a free play is created by both faculties, those of imagining and those of understanding. Consequently the sense of the sublime is awakened by a necessary stimulation resulting from sensitivity. The latter, plus the imagination, are then linked with a faculty higher than understanding, i.e., that faculty which sorts out problems without finding the solution to them. Kant calls this faculty Reason.

It is a faculty which legitimately seeks to know the principle and purpose of the universe and the destiny, origin and duration of the human soul. It seeks ultimately to know of the creator of nature and the soul. This faculty seeks to fathom ideas that cannot be conceptually determined, to summarize the primordial enigmas, the principles which wreak havoc on man's days on earth. It is reason which ponders the set of ideas causing man to inquire into the most problematic questions of life, and which find their summarizations within the domain of the soul of the subject, the world, the notion of divinity and of the infinite.

The sense of the sublime, however, intrinsically unites a datum of sensitivity (the rough ocean, the water spout, a mountain range, the deep trough of the ocean, the darkness of a moonless night, the desert at twilight) with an idea of reason producing a moral enjoyment in the subject, a point in which morality becomes pleasurable and where aesthetics and ethics reach their union and synthesis. Man finds in this synthesis motivation for his sentient activities, while granting to the rational idea, whose practical result was set forth by Kant in his *Critique of Practical Reason*, a foothold on which hinge image and experience. Man *feels* in himself his magnitude and his destiny, and at the same time his smallness (a mere feather blown by the wind of the universe in an infinite expansion). He feels sentiently that dignity which in the second critique has only been conceded as a "moral entity," wherein lies the sole link of moral sense and the idea of duty.

From the Sublime to the Sinister

The aesthetic sense will no longer remain, in Kant and after him, restricted to the limiting category of the beautiful. Objects which lack harmony and proper proportion among the elements in which they are included could enter the field of sensitivity, connecting this faculty with that of reason which is above the intellect. German idealism carried this Kantian incursion to the highest degree, which broadened the scope of the aesthetic, within the sphere that examines the sense of the sublime. The sentient presentation of the Rational Idea (Spiritual) was, for Hegel, who carried Kantian thought on aesthetics to its highest degree, the very limit of aesthetics. The beautiful and the sublime were synthesized in a unique category in which the sentient datum (and its limitation) and the infinite spirit are connected. Thereafter, the beautiful was conceived in such a way that inherent in it is found synthesized what Kant still differentiated as "beautiful" and "sublime." Beauty became divine presence, incarnation, revelation of the infinite in the finite. Schelling, Krause and Hegel together with the philosophers of nature and the romantics, would assume these premises as assumptions of their aesthetic thought. The beautiful would be the beginning, the initiation, the starting point of a journey toward the very heart of the divine. But that trip, through the dark jungle, was not free of danger and uneasyness. And the gloomy character of the hidden divinity only sensibly manifested itself through that which snatches us incessantly from the prison of our limitations, and would make poets and thinkers ask about the face of that veiled divinity. It is a tormented, contradictory divinity struggling to achieve its own identity from several points of view as we see in the writings of Hegel, Schopenhauer and the young Nietzsche. Could it be God or Satan who is revealed through that initiatory trip found in poetry and art? Could it be a splendid face like that luminous one that irradiated through three circles of lower hypostasis, that one which the

Renaissance artist Marsilio Ficino painted? Could it be a blinding light before which causes all to shield their eyes and which can be seen only in the shadows? Could it be the God of darkness, the heart of shadows, the obscure and sinister background of a tormented, broken-hearted deity, conceptualized as an entity of painfulness or as one of willfulness or a primordial oneness knowing only perpetual self-affliction? Or could that darkness be its ultimate veil, an anguished veil, which, like a dark night impedes the terminal flight, in the course of which one manages to overtake the prey? The anxiety which these questions cause opens the sensitive and intellectual curiosity toward what we perceive to be, from our limitation, something like a bottomless pit and we experience it as an essential vertigo. The presumably sinister aspect of the divinity thus invites the sentient thought to cause the category of the sinister to surpass that of the sublime.

In view of these considerations, Rilke's aphorism is fully justified: "The beautiful is the beginning of the terrible which we human beings can endure." And that beginning carries the temptation of our venturing toward the heart of the darkness, the source and origin, the place of mysteries, which should remain hidden but produce in us, on being revealed, the *sense* of the sinister.

. . . .

Thematic Inventory of Sinister Motifs

Kant, in his *Critique of Judgment*, sets the stage for romanticism. He opens the ideological nucleus which makes it possible.

Freud, in his beautiful book, *The Sinister*, recapitulates romanticism. He carries out a lucid thematic inventory of one of the most characteristic explorations of this movement: the sentient and conceptual determination of the sinister.

Freud associates with the term sinister the persons, things and situations which can be resumed as follows:

1. A sinister individual is the bearer of evil spells and of disastrous omens. To tangle with him brings some misfortune (failure in love, death, assassinations, madness).

2. A sinister individual, a bearer of evil spells and of disastrous omens for the subject, has or may have the character of his double or of some close relative (the father). The theme of the double is obviously associated, with the theme of the sinister.

3. "The doubt that an apparently animated being may really be alive and that, inversely, a lifeless object is animated in some form," e.g. wax figures or intelligent dolls that are automatons. Thus a woman whose beauty stems from that subtle point of union between the inanimate and the animate, as is

the case of a marble-like and frigid beauty, or like that of a statue despite the fact that a live woman is involved, or a painting that seems to have life to it. This ambivalence produces in the soul a feeling which suggests a profound, intrinsic and mysterious link between the familiarity and beauty of a face and the extraordinary magical, mysterious character which that totality of contradictions produces, that promiscuity between the organic and the inorganic, between the human and the inhuman. The final sensation does not fail to produce a certain very profound sinister effect which clarifies, in a disturbing way, the nature of artistic appearance and concomitantly some of the deepest dimensions of eroticism.

4. The repetition of a situation under conditions identical to the first time it was presented, as a genuine return to its first appearance, or a repetition which produces a magical and supernatural effect accompanied by the feeling of *déjà vu*, suggests a very pleasurable familiarity with regard to the one that is lived at that time (in case the repetition is only suspected), or rather a certain sensation of horror, fate and destiny (in case the repetition is flagrant).

5. Some images that allude to amputations or injury of bodily organs, which are most important and delicate like the eyes or the male member; in other words, those images which allude to lacerated and mangled parts of the body. These images produce a link between the sinister and the fantastic when the mutilated object is an apparently live being that seems human but is not. This is the case of the doll Olimpia in Hoffman's short story, "The Sand Merchant," cut to pieces by her creator. Separated members which are autonomized and achieve independent activity, e.g. feet that dance by themselves.

6. In general, Freud suggests that the sinister is found when the fantastic (what is dreamt up or desired by the individual in a hidden, veiled or self-censured form) is produced in reality, or when what is real assumes entirely the character of the fantastic. The sinister could be defined as the *absolute* fulfillment of a desire (essentially always hidden, forbidden, semi-censured). Freud alludes to a patient of his wife who, when a hotel guest had taken the room he has reserved exclaimed: "I hope he dies tonight!"--a wish that came true. The sinister character of Kurtz, the person sought by the narrator of Conrad's novel *The Heart of the Darkness*, arises from the fact that "that spirit who surfaced from nothingness" made all his dreams real, without censure or any elaboration, without any mediation between the fantastic and the real.

The sensation of the sinister comes about when the subject feels a foreboding about something, or fears and secretly desires something which suddenly becomes reality.

The feeling of the sinister produces then the fulfillment of a hidden, intimate and forbidden desire. A desire of one's unconscious fantasy which becomes a reality is sinister. It is the fulfillment of a fantasy formulated as desire although it is feared. In the gap between that desire and that fear lurks what is potentially sinister which, becomes effective when it comes into play. *Incarnate fantasy* could be the definitive formula of the sinister.

The sinister leads the individual to the source of fears and desires (which are interconnected): fear of castration in Freudian terms, fear of the desire to castrate one's rival (one's progenitor or brother). Sand thrown into one's eyes, a recurrent theme in Hoffman's short story "The Sand Merchant," would be expressive of the figurative use of that desire and that fear. The cutting into pieces of that automaton--the doll Olympia in Hoffman's story--would suggest the same ambivalent sentiment.

Hoffman's short story, "The Sand Merchant" constitutes in this sense, the most lucid inventory of romantic motifs of the sinister. We find in this story the six characteristics of the sinister previously set out.

. . . .

Inhospitable Familiarity of the Beautiful and the Sinister

Freud offers the following definition of the concept of the sinister: "The sinister in one's personal experience is present when *repressed* infantile complexes are revived by an exterior impression, or when primitive convictions that have been *overcome* seem to find a new confirmation." Something familiar and intimate is repeated which is forgotten through censure of the individual's conscience. When in this life something happens which serves to confirm those old abandoned convictions, we experience the sensation of the sinister and it is as if we said: "Just as if it is possible to kill another by the simple force of desire, it is possible that the dead may continue living and that they reappear in the places where they lived." In the sinister there seems to come about in reality a confirmation of the desires and fantasies which have been refuted by the clash of the individual with reality. As a result, we have immortality, the resurrection of the dead in this life, the product of pure thought, of real results without the mediation of activity.

In Hoffman's short story, the sinister is intrinsically articulated as a fulfillment of the fantastic. We see this in the doll Olympia, a blend of life and inert body; in the smashing of the doll, a brutal rupture of fiction which is thought to be real (and in making real a character more fantastic than fiction); in the repetition of the presence of the sand merchant, who is transformed into a seller of eyeglasses; in the repetition brought about by the subject in his adventure with Olympia apropos the renewal of his relationship with Clara, his former sweetheart; in the double of the sand merchant, the companion and collaborator of the subject's father and of the teacher who is the alleged father of Olympia. The whole narration is a continual bringing to the fore, by artistic means, of the sinister, but it is presented in such a way that the real and the fictitious are intertwined with such ambiguity--and wisdom--that the artistic effect is always preserved. Everything can be read as a double reading, according to a rational-realistic interpretation or a visionary-fantastic one, without either of them being able to arrogate to itself the full richness of the narration. The sinister is shown always veiled, hidden, in the form of absence, revolving about and seesawing in a spiral between reality and fiction and fiction and reality, never losing its perpetual to and fro motion. Our hypothesis on the articulation of the beauty and the sinister now becomes more defined.

In the beautiful we recognize perhaps a familiar face, recognizable, according to our limitation and stature, a being or object which we can recognize, which belongs to our home and domestic surroundings. It does not exceed our horizon. But, suddenly, what appears so familiar and harmonious regarding our own limitation reveals and brings mysteries and secrets which we have forgotten through repression, without being absolutely outside of the first fantasies which our desire contrived, a desire laden with primordial fears. That familiar presence, the doll Olympia, is presented to our eyes, identified through [the student] Nathaniel's eyes, as an emissary of forboding and fearful horrors, which may be secretly desired. That domestic presence, the father's friend and collaborator, the traveling seller of barometers and eyeglasses, suddenly reveals subterranean currents of our hidden criminal desires (to pull out our rival's eyes, to cast burning coals into the eyes of the father: a revelation masked in the inverted position of the patient subject and the executioner).

Provisional Conclusion

We can now round out and strengthen our hypothesis by defining what we consider to be the condition and limit of beauty: something sinister, of course, which just by being as it is, reveals a familiar face to us. The artistic work traces a hiatus between the pure repression of the sinister and its tangible and real presentation. It shows its necessary ambivalence in this. It suggests without showing, reveals without failing to hide something or to resort to chicanery, and shows as real something that shall crop up as fiction, which in the long run, shall come to be known as fiction of a lesser degree. In no case does it crudely make the sinister evident, for the artistic work would lack force if were it not for a premonition of the sinister. Without that presence--a veiled, suggested or metaphorized presence, in which the effect is expressed but the cause is concealed--art would lack vitality. What makes the work of art a "live form," according to Schiller's renowned definition, is that connivance and synthesis of desire's evil and obscure side and the veil in which it is woven and transformed, without it being completely out of sight. The sources of life are not repressed and, therefore, that apparently inert and inorganic form, like the doll Olympia, has full life and organicism, but in real life--art can never be realistic--the most secret desires of the species are not revealed or made known. Art transforms and transfigures those semi-secret and semi-forbidden desires which are eternally feared, it gives them a form or figure, thus preserving any source of vitality they have from which it follows that it is pertinent to speak of "veil" and "Mayan veil" to refer to the formal and outward appearance of the aesthetic work. It is a veil through whose orderly form "chaos must shine," as could be said by stretching Novalis' aphorism. The question that immediately comes to mind is: What is the ontological statute of that "veil" which is beauty? What is put in full view when that veil is removed and what is there behind the torn curtain?

Behind the curtain is the void, the primordial nothingness, the abyss which rises and inundates the surface (abyss is the dwelling place of Satan). Behind the curtain there are images that cannot be supported, in which are articulated before the hallucinating eye of the onlooker visions of castration, cannibalism, the ripping to pieces and resulting death; all of them presences in which the revolting, the disgusting, and that limit of the aesthetic summarized in Kant's *Critique* burst forth in all their splendid oral and excremental promiscuity. That ontological hole is thus full of cobwebs of images which reveal to the astonished and inexperienced eye of an infant the most horrible and hair-raising destructions, amputations and flayings. Can art, without mediation, show those images in all their crudeness of horror and nightmare? How, and under what mediating and transforming conditions, can it undertake to do so?

We can then formulate our hypothesis as follows:

1. The beautiful, without metonymical reference to the sinister, lacks the force and vitality to be able to be beautiful.

2. The sinister, if present without mediation or transformation (metaphorical and metonymical elaborations), destroys the aesthetic effect, and consequently its limiting boundary.

3. Beauty is always a veil, arranged in such a way that chaos must be presented behind it.

Art is fetishistic. It lies in the vertigo of the subject's position, who is on the verge of seeing that which cannot be seen, that vision which is blindness and which perpetually remains unchanged. It is as if art--the artist, his work, his characters, his spectators--put itself in a strange position, always last with regard to a revelation which is not fulfilled because it cannot be done. Therefore, there is no "last word" for the artistic work--nor is it possible to say any definitive word about it. It makes of that penultimate instant a space of rest and dwelling sufficient for the length of time that the fiction lasts.

[Translation of material from the First Part of the book *Lo bello y lo siniestro (The Beautiful and the Sinister)*, 2nd edition (Barcelona: Editorial Ariel, 1988)].

BIOGRAPHICAL SKETCH OF EDITOR

Donald W. Bleznick obtained his Ph.D. from Columbia University where he studied under Federico de Onís and Angel Del Río. He was a professor of Spanish literature at Ohio State University and Pennsylvania State University prior to assuming his professorship at the University of Cincinnati in 1967. He is the author or editor of 15 books on Hispanic Literature and over 80 scholarly articles which have been published in the United States, Mexico, Spain and Chile. From 1974 to 1983 he was editor-in-chief of *Hispania* and also served this journal as the associate editor of book reviews during the previous nine years. He was elected Vice-President (1992) and President (1993) of the American Association of Teachers of Spanish and Portuguese. Spain's Cruz de Caballero de la Orden de Mérito Civil (Knight's Cross of the Order of Civil Merit) was conferred on him in Madrid (1977). In that same year, a journal in The University of Salamanca named him one of the outstanding American scholars in the Hispanic field. He is a Fellow of the University of Cincinnati Graduate School and has won honors for his scholarship.